The Big Bang and the Holy Trinity

— PAUL COBB —

Sacristy
Press

Sacristy Press
PO Box 612, Durham, DH1 9HT

www.sacristy.co.uk

First published in 2024 by Sacristy Press, Durham

Copyright © Paul Cobb 2024
The moral rights of the author have been asserted.

All rights reserved, no part of this publication may be reproduced or transmitted in any form or by any means, electronic, mechanical photocopying, documentary, film or in any other format without prior written permission of the publisher.

Bible extracts, unless otherwise stated, are from the *New Revised Standard Version Bible: Anglicized Edition*, copyright 1989, 1995, Division of Christian Education of the National Council of the Churches of Christ in the United States of America. Used by permission. All rights reserved.

Every reasonable effort has been made to trace the copyright holders of material reproduced in this book, but if any have been inadvertently overlooked the publisher would be glad to hear from them.

Sacristy Limited, registered in England
& Wales, number 7565667

British Library Cataloguing-in-Publication Data
A catalogue record for the book is
available from the British Library

ISBN 978-1-78959-349-5

Man, dreame no more of curious mysteries,
As what was here before the world was made,
The first Mans life, the state of Paradise,
Where heauen is, or hells eternall shade,
For Gods works are like him, all infinite;
And curious search, but craftie sinnes delight.
              Fulke Greville, Lord Brooke
              (1554–1628), Sonnet LXXXVIII

. . . but, what the heck!

Contents

Preface... vi

Part 1. The Creator..1
In the beginning 1
God created 9
... the heavens.................................... 12
... and the earth 15
... and God said, "Let there be light"............... 17
... and God said, "Let the earth bring forth living
    creatures of every kind" 18
So God created humankind in his own image...... 25

Part 2. The creative potential....................37
In the beginning was the Word 38
... and the Word became flesh 43
... in him was life 46
... and the life was the light of all people 49
... he gave power to become children of God 51

Part 3. The creative force 55
A wind from God swept over the face of the waters . 56

... and I have filled him with the divine spirit......60
... you will be like God, knowing good and evil....67
... people began to call on the name of the LORD..70

Part 4. The end of creation......................81
For the first heaven and the first earth had passed away 82
I am the Alpha and the Omega 84
For as all die in Adam, so all will be made alive in Christ...89

Conclusion...................................92

Preface

Since the earliest times, humankind has been fascinated by the beauty and immensity of the universe. This has led to a deep desire to understand the origins of the awesome stage on which human lives are played. The earliest speculation on the beginnings of the universe was a religious enquiry that saw the hand of a supernatural entity in its creation. More recent times have offered new insights from observation of the natural laws that seem to govern the universe—the field of science.

The origins and nature of humanity itself are a natural part of this search, as humankind reaches out into the unknown to answer the "Why are we here?" question.

Many feel that scientific investigation has superseded religious insight as the way most likely to lead the human race to a true knowledge of its origin, and possibly its purpose. I am not one of them. Another camp regards scientific discovery as sometimes interesting, sometimes erroneous, but generally ineffective in describing matters of purpose and destiny, which are best left to religious enquiry. I am not a member of that group either.

The last centuries have seen these two approaches

increasingly at odds with each other and denying the other's validity and integrity. Even the more liberal adherents of these respective views see the two fields of enquiry as unconnected in any way, or *non-overlapping magisteria*, to quote the terminology of Stephen J. Gould. This school of thought advocates respectful non-interference between the realms of science and religion.

The separation of science and religion is not a good thing. It leads us to the situation where religions feel no pressure to review doctrine in the light of scientific discovery. When religion fails to interpret its historical message for the current age it deservedly loses its influence. The ridiculous movement to teach a literal biblical view of creation in some schools, despite the insights from palaeontology and evolutionary theory, is an example of what can happen when religion sees no need to embrace science. Science suffers equally from this false division. It cannot be denied that the first insights into the birth of the universe came from religious revelation, and, when allowance is made for the knowledge of the age, religious descriptions anticipated scientific theories by millennia. The scientific method is constrained by the natural world, but it is interesting to see how the word "God" creeps into the vocabulary of scientists as their investigations lead them closer to the moment the universe began.

The amazing progress of science has led to a sort of secular arrogance that presumes that humans, although they have supposedly arisen by chance as an artefact of the Big Bang, can ultimately discover the secret of life, the universe and everything if they don't wipe themselves out in the process. Religion requires us to acknowledge that creation was an act of God, and that true understanding will only follow when we use our God-given minds to investigate God's purpose in creation and when we open those same minds to dimensions beyond time and space. The truth revealed from religion opens up a creative and wonderful future for humankind that cannot be articulated through the language of science.

I'm appealing for an increasing overlap between these spheres of knowledge, so that each may be informed by the insights of the other and not be able to ignore uncomfortable discoveries in the other discipline. To help this along, this short book summarizes how comfortably the disciplines can sit together to provide a coherent and mutually enriching account of creation. I am particularly pleased with the insights into the difficult Christian doctrine of One God as three persons, the Holy Trinity, that come from embracing scientific discovery.

Although the religious thoughts come from my background as a Christian brought up in the Western tradition, I claim no exclusivity in the revelation of God for my own faith. The insights of Judaism, Islam and other deistic, and indeed non-deistic, faiths are best left to their adherents to document.

I have used the Christian Bible as the backbone for this study, which begins with the moment of creation.

PART 1

The Creator

In the beginning when God created the heavens and the earth, the earth was a formless void and darkness covered the face of the deep, while a wind from God swept over the face of the waters.

Then God said, "Let there be light"; and there was light.

And God said, "Let the earth bring forth living creatures of every kind."

Then God said, "Let us make humankind in our image, according to our likeness."

So God created humankind in his image, in the image of God he created them; male and female he created them.

Genesis 1:1,2,3,24,26,27

In the beginning

The ancient world of the Near East developed a rich mythology of the origins of the universe as the great thinkers of the time reached out into the unknown to explain the nature of the world around them. In seeking origins for the beauty, grandeur and menace of their world, they were also looking for an explanation of their place and purpose. The statement in the first verse of the Bible that "In the beginning God created the heavens and the Earth", written down in the sixth or seventh century BCE, was not a new idea even then. It could, perhaps, be considered more of an assertion by the Israelites in exile in Babylon that it was *their* God who was the Great Creator. I begin this account by exploring how the creation myth in the book Genesis relates to modern thinking on the origins of life. I am aware that some will already be offended by my assigning the Genesis creation story to the genre of "myth", but I hope that they will survive with my arguments long enough to realize that this terminology elevates rather than denigrates. The formulation of myths to explore the area outside of human knowledge allows the human intellect a much freer rein than the more trammelled demands of scientific reasoning. The first verse of Genesis, whatever its origins, encapsulates truths that the systematic approach of natural science was unable to postulate until 2,700 years later. These are that *there was a beginning*, and that *time began when the universe began.*

It has to be said that the Christian Church did not help the progress of scientific discovery by its adherence to a model of the universe with Earth at its centre and the observable heavenly bodies in a succession of spheres around it. This geocentric model was based on the thinking of Aristotle in the fourth century BCE as developed by Ptolemy in the second century CE, and was fairly successful in predicting the motions of the stars and the planets. It was also theologically convenient because it allowed room outside of the spheres for heaven and hell.

The Ptolemaic model spoke of a perfection and focus of creation, with Earth at its centre surrounded by the symmetry of spheres, and great courage was required by the scientists who were to come forward with alternative models in the sixteenth and seventeenth centuries CE. The penalties for religious unorthodoxy were extremely severe in those times, and promoting ideas considered to be heretical was not just a bad career move, but physically dangerous. A Polish priest, Nicolaus Copernicus (1473–1543), secretly circulated a model in which he proposed a solar system with the Sun at its centre and the planets in circular orbits. This model took nearly a hundred years to gather support, but it was, eventually, adopted by the Italian scientist Galileo Galilei (1564–1642) and the German astronomer Johannes Kepler (1571–1630).

Galileo demolished the Ptolemaic model when he constructed his telescope and observed four moons that circulated Jupiter. This demonstrated that not all heavenly bodies circulated the Earth. Johannes Kepler further undermined the model when he modified the Copernican theory to allow for planets to orbit the Sun in elliptical rather than circular paths.

Galileo and Kepler are key figures in the story of the relationship between science and religion. Galileo has been called the "father of modern science", and the parting of the ways between science and religion can be said to have its origins in his problems with the Catholic Church. He antagonized the Jesuits in the Collegio Romano with his acerbic criticism of their approach to science, but things really came to a head over his espousal of the Copernican heliocentric model of the universe. Unlike his ecclesiastical accusers, Galileo saw no conflict between the heliocentric model and biblical passages such as verse 5 of Psalm 104, which reads "You set the earth on its foundations, so that it shall never be shaken." Galileo followed Augustine's view that not all parts of the Bible were to be taken literally, particularly when the genre was clearly poetry, as in the book of Psalms. Galileo was a better scientist, and even theologian, than he was a politician. In the end, he offended too many powerful figures in the Church, and even upset his erstwhile supporter, Pope Urban VIII (1568–1644). He was found guilty of heresy by the Roman Inquisition, forced to recant and spent the rest of his life under house arrest. It took another 250 years for the Catholic Church formally to drop its opposition to the heliocentric model, but by then things were already moving on, as William Herschel's (1738–1822) observations showed the solar system to be moving through space.

Kepler, a Protestant who had studied at the University of Tübingen, had an easier time with the religious authorities when he authored the first published defence of the Copernican model. His later problems with the Church, when he defended his mother who was accused of witchcraft, were not related to his scientific work but were more a hazard of the age.

My own thoughts on the relationship between religion and science find their origins in Kepler's work. His search for a geometrical plan for the universe was inspired by his conviction that there was a connection between the physical and the spiritual, and that the universe itself was constructed in the image of God. In Kepler's theology, the Sun represented the Father, the stellar sphere the Son and the intervening space the Holy Spirit.

Despite the hindrance of dogmatism, science made its systematic and rigorous journey to arrive at the truth encapsulated in the first verse of the Bible. Even in the middle of the twentieth century, the prevailing theory was that the universe had always been there and was in a steady state of continuous creation without a beginning or an end. This theory, developed by Fred Hoyle (1915–2001) and others, withstood many observations, but the Big Bang theory, derived originally from Einstein's equations by the Belgian Roman Catholic priest Georges Lemaître (1894–1966), has now superseded the Steady State theory. The Big Bang theory predicted an event which brought the universe into being, and that the universe then underwent a rapid expansion. Science now agreed with the first verse of Genesis, that there was indeed a beginning.

The expansion of the universe was an observable phenomenon, and the American astronomer Edwin Hubble (1889–1953) was able to show that galaxies were moving away from each other by measuring the perceived increase in the wavelength of their light caused by the Doppler effect—the so-called red shift. This observation of the receding galaxies supported the Big Bang theory, a term which Hoyle himself coined as a sarcastic reference in a BBC Radio broadcast, but did not provide the final nail in the coffin of the Steady State theory. This was hammered home when the cosmic background microwave radiation predicted as a result of the Big Bang by George Gamow was accidentally discovered in 1964 by two young radio astronomers, Arno Penzias and Robert Wilson, using the Bell Laboratories equipment in New Jersey, USA.

The progress of science over the millennia has, through the Big Bang theory of cosmic origin, brought our scientific knowledge to the point where we understand that time could not exist before this event. This is a hard notion to grasp, as it seems to fly in the face of common sense. We are more disposed to think of time as a constant flowing stream that progresses in one direction wherever we are and whatever we are doing, and it enables us to think of events in terms of past, present and future.

This view of time is very much as described by Isaac Newton (1642–1727) in the late seventeenth century, who defined an "absolute, true and mathematical time [which] of itself, and from its own nature, flows equably without relation to anything external". This was the basis of Newton's laws of mechanics, from which he was able to predict the motion of the Moon and planets as well as the movement of objects on Earth.

Newton gave us the picture of the universe as a cosmic clockwork mechanism with every particle acting on every other component to create predictable rhythms and cycles. Newton's mechanics served science well and opened a path of discovery and prediction, but as a theory it had its limitations. The discrepancies created by this theory came to a head with the discoveries by Michael Faraday (1791–1867) and James Clerk Maxwell (1831–79) in the mid-nineteenth century in the fields of electricity, magnetism and optics. The new electromagnetic theories were spectacularly successful and ushered in the electronic age. They predicted a constant value for the speed of light, which did not depend on the speed at which the observer was moving. According to Newton, and the prevailing logic, light should reach an observer sooner if they were travelling towards the source or later if they were moving away.

This paradox was resolved in 1905 by Albert Einstein (1879–1955), then a young scientist working in the Swiss Patent Office in Bern. The solution was staggering in its concept and defied common sense, but it was soon confirmed by observation and experiment. While the speed of light remained constant, time and space were malleable. The equations of Einstein showed how time could not extend backwards beyond the point where the universe occupied no space. Science had arrived at the Genesis notion of the cosmic time clock starting to tick at the instant the universe came into being.

Science can now tell us so much more than the Bible of the immensity of this moment when the universe came into being. The scientific consensus is that this happened 13.7 billion years ago and began with tremendous release of uniform energy. Theories exist that can take us back to the tiniest fractions of a second after the emergence of this energy, and it is postulated that it was a tiny point which, still within the tiniest fraction of a second, underwent a dramatic expansion. It was during this period of expansion that it is thought that the irregularities occurred which would later allow the stars and galaxies to be formed as energy condensed into matter.

These amazing events revealed by science, and the sheer scale, complexity and beauty of the observable universe, must surely add to the sense of awe and wonder of those who seek the creator in their spiritual lives.

God created

The Big Bang theory of cosmic origin fits well with the traditions of Christianity, Judaism and Islam that God created the world out of nothing (*ex nihilo*). This was in contrast to the Ancient Greek tradition of a Demiurge, or craftsman, who fashioned the universe from pre-existing material, or chaos, which fits better with the science's discarded Steady State theory.

In fact, biblical texts can be quoted in support of both *ex nihilo* creation and creation by bringing order to chaos. The second verse of the Bible reads: "the earth was a formless void and darkness covered the face of the deep, while a wind from God swept over the face of the waters."

This could be read as God creating the world from pre-existing materials, but it may also represent God's involvement in the process of creation once begun, particularly in the context of the statement that God created the universe in the beginning in the first verse. The Hebrew word *reshit*, used in the first verse of Genesis, indicates that creation is not a one-off event, but is a starting point for a whole plan of action.

The texts supporting *ex nihilo* creation are much less equivocal and include the following extracts from the second book of Maccabees and the letter to the Hebrews:

> I beg you, my child, to look at the heaven and the earth and see everything that is in them, and

> recognize that God did not make them out of things that existed (2 Maccabees 7:28).
>
> By faith we understand that the worlds were prepared by the word of God, so that what is seen was made from things that are not visible (Hebrews 11:3).

The writer to the Hebrews is certainly right to say that belief in God as the creator is an act of faith, because science cannot help us here. The consequence of the Big Bang theory of the origin of the universe is that science does not exist outside of time, whereas theology has embraced the concept of a God who is outside of time since at least the fourth century CE. In Book XI of his *Confessions*, Augustine wrote of time being created at the moment of God creating the universe, and of the existence of God outside of time. He doubtless developed this view of God from the Platonic notion of true reality being eternal and unchanging. Augustine tackles the question of what God was doing before he created the universe, but dismisses this as a nonsensical question since the concept of "before" cannot exist outside of time.

Rational arguments from the physical nature of the universe for the existence of the creator have powerful counter-arguments. The Ancient Greeks saw the hand of the creator in the rational order of the universe, and, in the thirteenth century CE, Thomas Aquinas (1225–74) used this so-called teleological argument as one of his proofs for the existence of God. The modern manifestation of this view is the concept of intelligent design, which has grown in the latter part of the twentieth century. Intelligent design proposes that certain features of life and the universe can best be explained by an intelligent purpose rather than by a random process. An example of this is the "Goldilocks effect", where it is possible to consider a creator as an explanation for the fundamental forces of nature being "just right" for the universe to exist and for life to develop (though this is not necessarily intended). For instance, if the force of gravity were a little stronger, our Sun would burn more fiercely and have too short a lifetime to allow life to develop on Earth.

The concept of intelligent design can be countered by the anthropic principle and statistical arguments, such as the multiverse theory. The anthropic principle is that the universe appears "just right", because if it were otherwise then we would not be here to see it! We just happen to be in the right place at the right time. An extension of this is the multiverse theory which postulates an infinite number of universes with different characteristics and that we just happen to be in the one that allows human beings to come into existence.

It would seem that the rational arguments against a creator are becoming at least as speculative as those for a creator, and that these questions will only lead to further questions, such as "Was there a creator of the multiverse?" And all of this does not touch on the nature of the creator, and whether the creator is the one that people have for millennia called "God". The most convincing evidence for the existence of God would be to discover the purpose of the creator of the universe, and this is more likely to be found by looking to the future that creation has made possible for humankind.

The theological argument from Augustine gives God present at the moment of creation and raises the issue of the purpose of God in causing, shaping and projecting into the created universe. This is worth examining even if your belief doesn't extend beyond the limits of observation or you think that the universe, in all the awe-inspiring magnificence which science is revealing, just sort of happened.

... the heavens

The universe that we can see with the naked eye, and with the aid of telescopes and other scientific instruments that have been developed to help us to reveal its awesome size and magnificence, has come into existence due to the operation of the fundamental forces on the matter released by the Big Bang at the beginning of time. The sheer beauty of the night sky is profoundly moving. The dynamism at work in the galaxies, nebulae and stars and the diversity of cosmic objects still being discovered speak of the grandeur of creation.

The mechanism for the creation of the observable universe has been explored and, at a certain level, explained through scientific discovery in the latter part of the twentieth century and into the new millennium. The latest theories can relate the formation of stars and galaxies to the properties of matter and the fundamental forces that act upon it. Science has painstakingly revealed some of the rules that have brought about the universe as we experience it. At the moment of origin, the universe was homogeneous with all matter and forces indistinguishable from each other. Matter, at this time, could be considered as pure energy, and only later in the history of the universe does this start to condense into particles and objects with mass. The dual nature of matter as energy and mass was expressed in the most famous equation in the world, Einstein's $E=mc^2$, where E represents energy and m represents mass. The constant, c, is the speed of light.

As the universe expanded and cooled in those first billionths of a second of time, differentiation occurred and separate forces and classes of matter emerged. The quarks and leptons, which are the constituents of matter, formed new particles which associated in different ways to form the building blocks of the universe. As the expansion and cooling of the universe proceeded, new forces emerged which governed the formation and interaction of these particles.

The initial homogeneity of the universe at the point of creation began to break down during the period of cosmic inflation. Tiny perturbations appeared that eventually provided the seeds for matter to concentrate and then collapse to form stars and galaxies. As the plasma cooled, the fundamental particles combined and the universe became largely composed of protons, neutrons and electrons. This phase of the evolution of the universe was reached over a period of one second to three minutes after the Big Bang. After about 70, 000 years, the protons and neutrons had combined to form simple atomic nuclei, principally hydrogen ions, but also helium and traces of other nuclei. By 300,000 years, hydrogen and helium atoms had been formed by the capture of electrons. These atoms aggregated into giant molecular clouds. As far as is known, all stars were formed within these molecular clouds, which provided the lower temperatures and higher density needed to initiate a process whereby the cloud began to collapse inwardly under the influence of the fundamental force of gravity. This compression of hydrogen raised the temperature of the core of the forming star until the nuclear fusion process, which produces the energy of our own star—the Sun—was ignited. The core of the star released energy to counteract the gravitational force, and the new star became stable as these two forces reached equilibrium and further gravitational collapse was prevented.

Larger molecular clouds collapsed to form galaxies, and the gravitational force drew galaxies together in clusters and superclusters to give the universe the shape we observe today. Our knowledge of the structure of the universe and the lifecycle of stars has taken great leaps forward with the launch of the Hubble Space Telescope in 1990 and the James Webb Space Telescope in 2021, both producing stunning images that enable us to probe further and further back in time towards the Big Bang.

Stars undergo a lifecycle over billions of years, which leads to a death which is sometimes a slow cooling but may be, according to the size of the star, a spectacular explosion known as a supernova. Nuclear reactions occur within stars leading to the formation of heavier elements than hydrogen and helium, and these elements enrich the interstellar dust when the star emits matter during energetic phases of its cycle or at its demise in a violent explosion. Supergiant stars can collapse to form incredibly dense neutron stars. Colliding neutron stars are another source of heavy atoms to enrich the interstellar dust.

. . . and the earth

The next phase of evolution of our known universe is the formation of our Sun and its system of planets. The Sun was formed about 8 billion years after the Big Bang and incorporates the material generated in the nuclear factories of earlier generations of stars. The planets were formed by gravitational aggregation of the material left over from the formation of the Sun, which constituted the disc-shaped solar nebula.

Current theories suggest that there were initially five inner planets of the solar system, but that a Mars-sized object collided with the Earth resulting in the formation of the Moon. Our own planet is about 4.5 billion years old and was initially molten, but the outer layer of the planet cooled as water accumulated in the atmosphere, giving the Earth a solid crust. Condensing water accumulated on the surface, and this may have been supplemented by ice from colliding comets to form the oceans. Gases released by volcanic activity helped to form the atmosphere.

The cooling crust of the Earth, the lithosphere, consisted of a number of tectonic plates, and by 3.5 billion years ago the Earth's magnetic field was formed, helping to prevent the atmosphere being stripped away by the solar wind, a stream of high-energy charged particles emitted by the Sun.

The shape and position of the continents has been moulded by the tectonic plates drifting over the more-fluid asthenosphere on which they "float". Mountain ranges have formed where tectonic plates have collided. The highest mountains on Earth, the Himalayas, are formed from rock uplifted by the collision of the Indo-Australian and Eurasian tectonic plates. To give some idea of the timescales involved, the Indo-Australian plate is moving at 67 mm per year, which leads to the Himalayas rising by about 5 mm per year. Hardly a good reason to rush to climb Mount Everest as soon as possible! Other familiar geological processes such as sedimentation, volcanic activity, marine erosion and weathering have contributed to making this amazingly diverse and beautiful planet where life could begin. Some of the more spectacular scenery, such as the Norwegian fjords and lakes, has been sculpted by the action of glaciers during periodic glacial periods, when the Earth's temperature has fallen. The last of these peaked about 20,000 years ago, when ice sheets covered large parts of the North American and Eurasian continents. Geological processes have built the Earth that we know over its 4.5-billion-year history and continue today as we see volcanoes and the action of the sea continually reshape the land.

. . . and God said, "Let there be light"

It is natural to think of light present in the universe from the moment of the Big Bang, but, in fact, a period of darkness ensued that lasted for several million years. After this time, the first stars burst into life, illuminating the universe. These first stars were much bigger and brighter than those we observe in our part of the universe, with masses of a thousand times the mass of our Sun.

The very first light of the universe is believed to have been captured by the NASA Spitzer Space Telescope.

This light was originally in the visible and ultraviolet wavelengths, but it has been observed as the lower-energy infrared light as its wavelength has been stretched on the long journey through expanding space.

The Genesis vision of that first light introduces the idea of God creating through utterance, and the form of "And God said ... " begins to be used as God's word shapes creation. This impression of God directing the process of creation counters the view from Deism that God does not intervene in the progress of creation and allows it to run according to the laws of nature established at the moment of creation.

This is an important distinction because the Christian, Jewish and Islamic view of a God, who we know through revelation, requires the continuing involvement of God in creation. The notion of a God who continues to be involved with creation causes us to consider how that God may be accessible to us in our daily lives.

... and God said, "Let the earth bring forth living creatures of every kind"

The physical universe has been created through the development of increasing complexity from its origin in the simplicity of pure energy. This has led to that most complex artefact of creation, which we call "life". The Genesis account continues from the creation of the heavens and the Earth to the creation of living organisms: vegetation on the third day, sea creatures and birds on the fifth day, and animals on the sixth day.

The fields of science defined by physics serve the investigation of the nature of matter and its fundamental interactions, but the disciplines of chemistry have advanced knowledge of the interactions of the elements that have arisen from hydrogen and helium in the burning cores of stars. Chemistry has revealed laws which explain and predict the complexity of these interactions and how they relate to the structure of atoms at the level of protons, neutrons and electrons. The field of organic chemistry has helped advance knowledge of the intricate structures that can be built on a skeleton of carbon atoms, and the molecules thus formed are basic components of life. Life is another order of complexity, which the biological sciences explore.

There are a number of theories in science concerning the origin of life on Earth, but they all involve the formation of chemical building blocks that combined to produce molecules of greater complexity which eventually became self-replicating organisms. It was Charles Darwin (1809–82) who, in 1871, first proposed that this process may have begun in a "warm little pond, with all sorts of ammonia and phosphoric salts, lights, heat, electricity, etc. present, [so] that a protein compound was chemically formed ready to undergo still more complex changes". This was first investigated experimentally by Alexandr Ivanovich Oparin (1894–1980), who concluded that a primaeval soup of organic molecules could be formed in the oxygen-less atmosphere of the primitive Earth through the action of sunlight. A famous experiment conducted in 1953 by Stanley Miller, a graduate student, demonstrated that simple amino acids could be formed from methane, ammonia and hydrogen, and water by the action of an electric spark, which was used to simulate lightning in the atmosphere of the early Earth. Miller and his professor, Harold Urey, found the presence of 13 of the 22 amino acids which combine to form the proteins found in living organisms.

The next stages of the development of life are the combination of the small molecules, or monomers, to form long chains, or polymers, and the organization of these molecules into the precursors of living cells. Life could not begin until there was a chemical sequence that enabled a system of chemical compounds to reproduce itself. There are several theories as to how this sequence could occur, but laboratory experiments have, so far, failed to simulate the conditions necessary. The difficulties are almost certainly due to the huge timescale over which the chemical reactions took place and the wide variety of conditions under which many chemical transformations were made. These may have included extraterrestrial conditions, as it is feasible that the "primaeval soup" was enriched with material from bodies colliding with the early Earth.

Once primitive life was present on Earth, ongoing creation demanded a mechanism whereby it could increase in complexity, and this mechanism was discovered in the theory of evolution. Evolution is a process that enables a life form to undergo changes that cause it to adapt to, and flourish in, its environment. This theory proposes that all life forms have evolved from common ancestry over billions of years.

The theory of evolution was first proposed in 1858 in separate papers to the Linnaean Society in London by the naturalists Charles Darwin and Alfred Russel Wallace (1823–1913). The following year Darwin published his detailed support of the theory in his book *On the Origin of Species*, which was based on his observations of the complexity of life demonstrated by the diversity of life forms. Darwin's book introduced the concept of natural selection as the mechanism by which life could evolve; indeed the full title of his book was *On the Origin of Species by Means of Natural Selection, or the Preservation of Favoured Races in the Struggle for Life.*

Natural selection is the process that enables a trait in an organism which confers an advantage to be propagated in subsequent generations until it becomes widespread in a reproducing group of organisms. This occurs because the organisms with the favourable trait are more likely to survive and reproduce. When this happens over many generations, it can lead to the emergence of different species.

Darwin's theory had no mechanism for the inheritance of characteristics from a previous generation, but this was provided in 1865 by the Austrian-Czech friar and scientist Gregor Mendel (1822–84). Mendel showed that traits were inherited in a predictable manner and gave Darwin's theory the mechanism that it needed. Mendel conceived the idea of heritable traits from studying over 21,000 hybrid pea plants and concluded from his analysis that units of inheritance from the male and female parent combined to produce a characteristic of the offspring.

The means by which information was passed from one generation to the next in Mendelian inheritance was revealed by the discovery in 1944 of DNA as the material constituting genes and chromosomes by Oswald Avery and his co-workers Colin MacLeod and Maclyn McCarty. The way that this information was encoded by DNA became apparent from the x-ray crystallographic work of Rosalind Franklin at King's College London and enabled James Watson and Francis Crick, at the Cavendish Laboratory, Cambridge, to publish the double-helix structure of DNA in 1953.

This view of DNA as two connected strands linked by nucleotide bases showed how genetic information could be reproduced. DNA contains four nucleotide bases, designated A, T, C and G. The sequence of these units along a strand of DNA is the encoded information of inheritance. The way that the two strands of DNA are linked by these bases is important because, as James Watson discovered, C can only link to G, and A only to T. This means that each strand, if separated, contains the information to build the complementary strand of DNA.

The concept of evolution of simple structures into more complex systems has been in the history of human thought since the earliest Greek philosophers, such as Anaximander (c.610–c.546 BCE), and it is worth considering why it took so long for this to be developed into a theory on the development of life. Some might want to blame it on restrictive Church teaching, but this is probably not the main cause. There is no doubt that Darwinian evolution causes problems to many Christians who understand the words of the Bible in a literal manner, and the debate in the USA over what should be taught in schools shows that the controversy Darwin caused still rages. Perhaps the best explanation for the comparatively recent emergence of the theory of evolution is the sheer timescale over which the process of natural selection operates. The first simple cells existed 4 billion years ago, and it took 3.5 billion years for multi-cellular organisms and the simplest animals to appear. The land plants made on the third day of creation in Genesis emerged 475 million years ago; the sea creatures of the fifth day 500 million years ago; and the land animals of the sixth day date from about 300 million years ago. Processes that operate over these timescales are hard for the human mind to imagine, just as is the vast scale of the universe. Our minds are accustomed to dealing with quantities that relate to our daily experience and our lifespan, and things that operate in orders of magnitude outside of our experience are counter-intuitive.

Natural selection is worth looking at in further detail as it provides a way of observing creation in action. It occurs because changes in the *genotype*, that is the nature and organization of genes in the chromosomes, can lead to changes in the *phenotype*, which is the physical effect in the organism. Traits such as size, hair colour and behaviour, for example, in a human, combine to make the phenotype. A new trait may be the result of a change in a single gene, but it is more likely to be the result of variation in a number of genes. Natural selection works through the way changes in the phenotype affect how an organism can individually and collectively flourish in its environment. Changes in a trait which will enhance the ability of an organism to survive and reproduce in its environment will cause the new trait to accumulate in a population because those individuals bearing the trait will have more descendants.

The process of natural selection uses the creative potential of a system that generates many possibilities, such as the genotype, in a situation where the results of its changes, in this case the phenotype, compete for resources in a common environment. There is a narrower view of the mechanism of creation in the gene-centred view proposed by the American biologist George C. Williams and expanded and popularized by Richard Dawkins in his 1976 book, *The Selfish Gene*. Dawkins seeks to illustrate a gene-centred view of evolution by describing how genes act only to replicate themselves in future generations and that this "selfish" mechanism drives the process of natural selection. A broad view of evolution as a mechanism of creativity can accommodate a "selfish gene" as a driver of natural selection, but the gene-centred perspective is an intellectual cul-de-sac for those unable to reach out for a direction and a purpose in creation.

So God created humankind in his own image

Genesis tells us that God created human beings, male and female, on the sixth day, and that humans were the culmination of his creative work made to fill the Earth as the dominant life form. Humankind has certainly carried out God's commission, using the world's natural resources so that the human race may flourish and increase. The twentieth century has brought startling evidence from environmental science of the effect that the development of human prosperity can have on the Earth, and there is a growing awareness of the responsibility to preserve life on Earth that comes with the dominion over the Earth granted by God in the Genesis account of creation.

The theology of the early Church explored the concept of humans being created in the image of God. The terms "image" and "likeness" were distinguished, and theologians such as Irenaeus (*c.*130–*c.*202 CE) and

Origen (*c.*185–*c.*253 CE) regarded "image" as referring to the original condition of human beings which was destined to become the glory of humanity's final state of "likeness" to God. The influence of Platonic thinking that the goal of human beings is to become the likeness of God is apparent here, and this idea offers a direction and purpose to human existence.

Reading the story of human creation from science is an essay in probability. From the sub-atomic world of wave mechanics through to the macro scale of the evolution of stars, planets and life itself, change and chance follow laws based on statistical theory. The processes of creation and the laws that govern them are characterized by immense numbers and long timescales. These reduce the significance of individual data points as the variations are lost within the averages of huge sets of data.

When cold statistics are applied to studies of humanity, a human being is reduced to a single datum in a huge population set, and it is very easy to lose sight of the uniqueness and importance of the individual. Even in the medical sciences, the treatment of an individual is based on principles derived from the general characteristics of human beings. New medicines for example are evaluated statistically, and a medicine judged as efficacious can be ineffective or even toxic when given to a particular individual. The social consequences of de-individualization of human beings are particularly dangerous. Sub-groupings are formed, and stereotypes applied to them. The consequent de-personalization paves the way for many evils ranging from social exclusion to genocide.

In all this, Christianity preserves the importance of the individual in our perception of the enormity of our environment. When the psalmist says "I praise you, for I am fearfully and wonderfully made" (Psalm 139:14a), it is an assertion of his own uniqueness and significance. Jesus took this a step further when he taught that " ... even the hairs of your head are all counted" (Matthew 10:30). The statement in Genesis that "God created humankind in his own image" offers the Christian a perspective on the large stage on which the drama of creation is being enacted that focuses on human beings as individual players on that stage as they relate to their creator in ongoing creation. But it isn't as easy as that! Christianity opens up a new concept of humanity as passing through individuality to an eternal unity with the creator, so it will be necessary to explore, before too long, the implications of this teaching if we are to begin to understand the truth about human creation.

Individuality is something we experience on a daily basis, to the point where we accept as a matter of fact that each person is a distinct individual. Where people appear physically similar, it is considered to be a strange phenomenon, and we find "lookalikes" amusing and entertaining. Even with twins we accept that the similarities between people do not smother the flame of individuality of each sibling. Our instinctive understanding of individuality is supported by our increasing knowledge of the chemical and biological make-up of the human body. An example of a biological trait that has been used as a mark of individuality is the human fingerprint. Although the forensic use of fingerprints in criminal detection dates only from the late nineteenth century, there is a long history of using the distinctive pattern of ridges on the fingers as a means of identification of an individual. Chinese merchants of the eighth century CE authenticated documents for loan contracts with fingerprints, and there is archaeological evidence of parties to legal contracts in Babylon in the nineteenth century BCE impressing their fingerprints into the clay tablets of the documents.

Our knowledge of the chemical basis of biological individuality followed from the discovery of the giant molecule, DNA, as the means of shaping and passing on to a new generation human traits such as stature and skin colour. DNA is present in every living cell of the body, and each individual has a unique variation of the DNA structure. The twentieth century CE saw the most amazing development of human knowledge of their genetic make-up when it became possible to explore the composition of DNA and relate this to the chemical mechanisms in the body which led to the development of biological traits. For instance, it became possible to identify the parts of the DNA molecule which determine eye colour.

I have described DNA as a giant molecule: it would be more accurate to describe it as a polymer, which is a large molecule made up of repeating units. The entire human DNA, or the genome, as it is known, consists of approximately 3 billion units. The genome can be considered as a blueprint for the individual, as it contains all of the information needed to determine physical make-up. In humans, the DNA is found in 46 long pieces, known as chromosomes, which organize themselves as 23 pairs. Not all of the length of the molecule is involved directly in the body chemistry. Certain areas, though, contain the coded information to make proteins, and these areas, varying widely in their length, are known as genes.

Science has provided a good explanation of how the characteristics of an individual are a consequence of the DNA structure, or to use scientific terminology, how the phenome relates to the genome.

DNA contains coded information for the production of proteins, and the code is held in the repeating units of its structure. The precise sequence of Guanine, Thymine, Cytosine and Adenine (G, T, C and A) along the giant DNA chains is known as the genetic code. The genes, through a process of transcription, copy information on the DNA sequence to a similar molecule called RNA. In a part of the cell called a ribosome, the RNA information is used to make amino acids, which are the building blocks of proteins. The information from RNA enables proteins to be made from specific amino acids assembled in a defined order by the process of translation. These proteins are intimately involved in the body chemistry and give rise to individual characteristics.

A huge step in our understanding of the biological source of individuality came from the Human Genome Project, which was initiated in the USA under the leadership of Dr James Watson in 1990. Its principal goals were to identify the 3 billion base pairs of human DNA and the 20,000 to 25,000 genes. Major funding came from the US government and, in the UK, the Wellcome Trust through its support of the Sanger Institute in Cambridge. The goals were achieved in 2003, and there is now a database of information on the human genome available in the public domain. The success of the project was announced jointly by the then US President Bill Clinton and the then British Prime Minister Tony Blair in 2000, when the first draft of the human genetic sequence was published. This project was an awe-inspiring feat of international scientific cooperation and human ingenuity, and the database that has resulted will feed research into many areas of understanding, leading to improving human life. In the field of medicine, knowledge from the human genome will lead to a new generation of drugs that can be directed to specific genetic dysfunction to replace the scatter-gun treatment of diseases defined by symptoms. Also patients will be treated according to their genetic make-up and not on the assumption that they will respond to treatment the same as an "average person".

The potential for scientific knowledge and human progress in the human genome database is only just beginning to be mined, but what does this database tell us about human individuality? Conventional wisdom has been that human beings share a DNA pattern that is of the order of 99.9 per cent identical. This was deduced from observations of spot differences in the genome where genes differ between individuals by just one of the repeating units. This type of variation is known as an SNP (single nucleotide polymorphism), and the variants produced are alleles. More recent work, however, has shown that there is a complex higher-order architecture of the human genome. This higher architecture allows for much more genetic variety between individuals, and also increases the genetic distance between humans and apes. A major source of the individuality of a human being is the number of copies of certain segments of DNA in the genome. It is now known that more than 10 per cent of the 20,000 to 25,000 genes contain variations in the number of copies of sections of DNA, and that these copy number variations (CNVs) affect a wide range of individual characteristics, including susceptibility to disease. More than 10 per cent of CNVs can be attributed to variations between races and show how human beings have adapted to their environment since their common ancestry in Africa 50,000 years ago.

The genetic variation between individuals shows adaptations to the environment, and they can be seen as a window on the continuing biological evolution of the species.

So, is evolution a mechanism that has made us in the image of God, and one that will carry us forward to become the likeness of God? *Homo sapiens* is distinguished from the other animals by the ability and inclination to acquire knowledge and develop wisdom, a capacity that we can call "sapience". The emergence of sapience as more complex animals evolved was a key milestone on the road of evolution. With humanity's ability to reason and enquire into their origin and purpose came the possibility of being able to shape their own destiny. The ability to make informed choices based on accumulated wisdom has to be a comparatively new vehicle for the continuing work of creation. The choices that human beings make can be powerful indeed and affect the future not just of the human race, but also the future of the planet Earth. The creative power of the human race is, perhaps, the distinguishing feature that identifies us as being made in the "image of God". Other animals can be considered as builders and, therefore, creators, but human creativity is special. It is creativity with direction and vision, and it is creativity inspired by God and in partnership with God.

The choices that we make enable humans to evolve from the image of God into the likeness of God. We can, of course, make the wrong choices, and the catalogue of some of the worst ones is recorded in the history of our race. What distinguishes a right choice from a wrong choice is the effect that it has on the forward movement of humanity in the direction of becoming the likeness of God. The issue of human choice and divine purpose is tackled in the second account of creation in the book Genesis which tells the story of how the first humans, Adam and Eve, made a choice to go against the way that the Creator was leading them. The consequences of the wrong choice are allegorized in the story of the "Fall" and are grave indeed. Adam and Eve are booted out of paradise and the presence of God, and are condemned to lives of pain and hardship ending in death.

The doctrine of a "fall from grace" has been a powerful part of Christian theology since the days of the Early Church. Augustine was responsible for articulating the doctrine of "original sin", which declared that Adam's wrong choice had consequences that were inherited by subsequent generations. This meant that humankind was doomed to make the wrong choices leading to its destruction and could only be saved from this fate by the grace of God. The Latin Church Father Augustine of Hippo (354–430) followed the teachings of Paul that "Adam brought death into the world".

There were other interpretations of the biblical allegory in the Early Church, particularly among the Greek Fathers such as Origen and Irenaeus, but these were overshadowed by the huge influence of Augustine, which survives to this day.

It has to be faced, however, that the doctrine of the Fall doesn't fit at all well with the theory of evolution, the observation of continuing creation and the concept of humankind growing into the likeness of God. Since the Fall works in the opposite direction of human progress, another doctrine was needed by theologians to get things moving in the right direction. The image of God was restored through the concept of atonement, in which humanity is rescued from the consequences of the Fall and put back on the path which leads to its amazing destiny by the intervention of the Creator. The doctrines of the Fall and atonement are useful models in understanding the relationship between God and humankind, but the observations of natural science make the doctrine of a Fall look a bit shaky and atonement like a patch on a dodgy argument.

A more cohesive account of the work of the creative process can be developed through returning to the thoughts of the Greek Fathers of the Early Church. Irenaeus, writing towards the end of the second century CE, was influenced by Stoic and Platonic ideas as well as by the theology of John's Gospel. He argued that human beings were not made immortal and incorruptible but with potential to become so. Coming to an understanding of "good", which comes from obeying God, and "evil", which arises from disobedience, can only be achieved through experiencing both.

I'd like to avoid the pejorative term of "sin" in paraphrasing Irenaeus's argument. Sin is just a word for making the wrong choice, and "evil" is the consequence of this, whereas "good" arises from making the right choices. Making the right choices keeps us in harmony with the creative flow, which is the direction of our destiny. The wrong choices move us away from God and in the direction of oblivion. This mechanism works both individually and collectively for humanity, and the perspective from Irenaeus permits us to see the free will of humans as an instrument for continuing creation with the ability to move humankind towards its great destiny. The mythology of the Fall helps us to understand the consequences of opposing the direction of creation, while Redemption shows us that the Creator makes a way back possible.

From this, I conclude that Darwinian evolution was the mechanism by which we were formed in the image of God, but that a new dimension of evolution is required to continue human progress until we become the likeness of God. The emergence of sapience in evolution was our "Garden of Eden moment", and since that time Darwinian evolution has ceased to be the driver of human progress.

The key to this new dimension of human development must be in the potential for evolution held in the natural laws and physical constants that existed at the moment of creation. The next section of this book will look at the observed order in the universe, and particularly how this relates to the human experience.

PART 2

The creative potential

In the beginning was the Word, and the Word was with God, and the Word was God. He was in the beginning with God. All things came into being through him, and without him not one thing came into being. What has come into being in him was life, and the life was the light of all people. The light shines in the darkness, and the darkness did not overcome it.

There was a man sent from God, whose name was John. He came as a witness to testify to the light, so that all might believe through him. He himself was not the light, but he came to testify to the light. The true light, which enlightens everyone, was coming into the world.

He was in the world, and the world came into being through him; yet the world did not know him. He came to what was his own, and his own people did not accept him. But to all who received him, who believed in his name, he gave power to become children of God, who were born, not of blood or of the will of the flesh or of the will of man, but of God.

> *And the Word became flesh and lived among us, and we have seen his glory, the glory as of a father's only son, full of grace and truth.*
>
> **John 1:1–14**

In the beginning was the Word

These opening words of the Gospel of St John, written around the beginning of the second century CE, not only pave the way for Augustine's later assertion of God being outside of time, but they introduce the concept of the "Word" as the creative facet of the nature of God. John's opening statement closely parallels the first verses of the Bible and may be viewed as an updating of the Genesis account of creation, influenced by reflection on the life and teachings of Jesus of Nazareth.

John's concept of "the Word", or *logos* in the original Greek text, has deep roots in Greek philosophy. From as early as the fifth century BCE, Heraclitus used *logos* to link rational discourse with the natural order of the world. Plato, Aristotle and, particularly, the Stoics saw the presence of a deity in the rational world order. The writer of John's Gospel is inviting us to examine how God, present at the moment of creation, is imposing a rationality and order to the emerging cosmos. The parallel to this in Genesis is the more pictorial language of God's creating by utterance ("And God said 'Let there be light.'" Genesis 1:3), but John's development of the theology opens a path to consider what the Word may mean in terms of initiating and shaping the universe.

The *logos* idea proposes a set of basic rules which govern the emergence of the universe, and that these rules derive from the nature of God. The created universe emerges as a reflection of the image of the creator, through a projection of the creator from timelessness into time, as we read in Psalm 19, "The heavens are telling the glory of God; and the firmament proclaims his handiwork." The "Word of God" brings order to the universe, and science is revealing the physical nature of this order and the intricacy of the building blocks, physical constants and rules on which creation is based. The true creative potential of the Word of God, however, can only be revealed by considering the history of creation and the possibilities that continuing creation offers.

If the "Word of God" represents the creative potential present at the beginning of time, then the physical structure of creation is found in the nature of matter and the fundamental forces that act upon it. Four fundamental forces are known to science, which are referred to as the weak interaction, the strong interaction, electromagnetism and gravity.

The idea of all matter being composed of fundamental particles was explored as the philosophical concept of atomism, and dates back at least as far as the fifth century BCE with Leucippus and Democritus. The Epicurean atomism of the early third century BCE distinguished between fundamental particles and indivisible magnitudes, and this doctrine was revived in European thought in the first half of the seventeenth century CE by the French Catholic priest Pierre Gassendi, who modified the ancient model with the insights of Christian theology. Incidentally, Gassendi was one of the defenders of Galileo when his observations on the nature of the solar system brought him into conflict with the Church.

The scientific discovery of fundamental particles really began with John Dalton (1766–1844), an English scientist and Quaker, in the nineteenth century. Dalton proposed that each element in nature was composed of fundamental and indivisible particles that he called "atoms".

It could be said that Dalton's Atomic Theory, published in 1803, marked the end of alchemy and the beginning of chemistry as it established the basis of the composition of all materials. However, near the end of the century, it was discovered that atoms were not the fundamental particles of nature, but they were in turn built up of even smaller constituents. Ernest Rutherford (1871–1937), a New Zealand-born chemist and physicist working at the Cavendish Laboratory in Cambridge, discovered that the atom consisted of a small positively charged nucleus surrounded by a diffuse cloud of negatively charged electrons. The Danish scientist Niels Bohr (1885–1962) proposed that electrons were limited to special orbits around the nucleus which gave them specific energies.

The discoveries of nuclear physics and quantum mechanics in the twentieth century led to greater understanding of the structure of atoms, to the point where it became possible to release huge amounts of energy from the atom by the process of nuclear fission. This permitted the development of nuclear weapons as well as providing a means of generation of electricity. The middle of the twentieth century brought the discovery of a confusing array of particles created by experiments in nuclear fission and the induced collision of particles in huge accelerators, but some order was brought to this by the development of the Standard Model, which recognized 24 fundamental particles and predicted the existence of another, the Higgs boson. The Higgs boson was, after a forty-year search, identified in 2012 in an experiment in the Large Hadron Collider. This model is by no means the last word, as scientists continue to investigate the relationship between the forces that govern the interaction between fundamental particles, with a view to a theory that unites these forces.

Fusion of Christian thought and scientific theory explains the creative power in the *logos*, the Word spoken by God in creation. The Word expressed in the fundamental natural laws at the moment the universe began reveals its continuing power as systems of increasing complexity emerge. The evolution of the universe from a homogenous point of energy to the unimaginably large and magnificent structure that we can observe today stands as evidence of this creative power.

It is not just the arrangement of matter that becomes more complex as creation proceeds: more detailed natural laws are also needed to define the emerging complexity. It may be flippant to say that Archimedes' Principle was not needed until the bathtub was invented, but I think you'll follow the train of thought. All of the laws of chemistry were irrelevant until elements were formed in the universe, but the potential for them lay within the fundamental laws present at the moment of creation.

This begins to define ongoing creation in terms of the generation of ever more complex systems discoverable through the natural laws that govern them. As the human mind engages with this complexity and discovers these laws, new disciplines of learning develop to drive human understanding forward. There is, however, a negative side to subdivision of learning into disciplines, as specialism becomes the sire of many other *isms*. Philosophy and theology are no less prone to this problem than science. A compartmentalized approach to acquiring knowledge requires regular holistic review if knowledge is to grow into wisdom, but specialism provides a barrier to this intellectual necessity. You may think that, at this point, I'm about to bang on about the division between science and religion again, but I'll spare you that—for now!

... and the Word became flesh

I have used the metaphysical image, deriving from Genesis, of human beings created in the image of God with the opportunity to become the likeness of God. In being the image of God, we have the ability to create things that we know to be "good", and in doing so we begin to fulfil our full potential. That potential is limited only by the boundaries of the Word of God, and in fulfilling our potential we become united in the Word of God. This concept is quite difficult to comprehend as it stretches us beyond our experience, but an event in human history has helped advance our understanding of our potential to become united in the Word of God. A person was born who was fully the Word of God, and the opening of John's Gospel tells how the Word of God became a human being in the person of Jesus of Nazareth. Such a person was anticipated by the Old Testament scriptures, but these references were only properly understood in hindsight after reflection on the life, death and resurrection of Jesus.

This wonderful event in the history of the universe became possible through the emergence of sapience in evolution and the consequent ability of the human mind to interact with God. Once the ability to seek God had developed, humankind became a partner in the ongoing process of creation with the ability to shape its direction through the choices made by individuals. *Homo sapiens* was formed in a mould that was shaped by the Word of

God, the physical laws of the universe. This prepared the way for the next stage of evolution of the species, which would be through reaching out to dimensions outside of time and space, in order to gain what we might call spiritual maturity. The birth of Jesus Christ brought into the world a person who was fully human, but also spiritually mature to the extent of being in unity with God. As such Jesus represents the fulfilment of the potential of humankind; he is the "Word made flesh".

Jesus of Nazareth was a person who during his life on Earth made choices that were aligned with the direction of creation and were, therefore, creative and "good". He sought to teach others to do likewise and denounced those who misled people into making the wrong choices. He taught that, although making the wrong choices caused an individual to be in disharmony with the creative flow, acknowledgment that the choice was wrong and learning from error could restore a harmonious relationship. He expressed this in terms of God forgiving the sins of those who repented.

Just as ignoring the law of gravity can bring fatal consequences, so can a failure to understand the need to live in harmony with the flow of creation that comes from the Word of God. Science and philosophy have led Western society to an age of materialism where reality is confused with tangibility. Spirituality is treated with suspicion and even hostility in an increasingly secular society. In the minds of many, it is not so much the highest domain of human enquiry and experience as an assembly point for charlatans. Organized religion must take responsibility for this through its inability to respond to developments in philosophy and science and its failure to modernize sufficiently its language and message. The value of ancient wisdom is rapidly reduced if it is not interpreted afresh by each generation.

The interaction of the human mind with God not only guides the choices that individuals make, but it also can be seen as the origin of religious laws and moral and ethical codes. These are no less the Word of God than the fundamental physical laws of the universe. The Ten Commandments given to Moses by God on Mount Sinai defined the behaviour that would ensure harmony between human choices and the direction of creation. Unfortunately, once these laws governing human behaviour are written down, they start to lose their value because they replace the interaction of the human mind with God. In Jewish history, the Ten Commandments became rapidly expanded into many arcane rules and laws, and people sought a relationship with God through strict adherence to these scriptures—the Torah. The teaching of Jesus sought to reclaim the role of the human mind in this relationship. Jesus taught in parables that made people think, and his outspoken opposition to those who sought God solely through the rule book led ultimately to his execution at the request of the religious authorities.

... in him was life

The development of laws and codes of behaviour is analogous to the emergence of natural laws in that they arise from the progress of creation through evolution. Just as the increasing complexity of the universe required whole new sciences with their associated laws to define the behaviour of matter, so, as human interactions and society became more complex, maintenance of harmony with the creative direction required a more complex approach to the rules governing human behaviour. Jesus did not advocate the abolition of the Law of Moses; instead he wanted the full power of the Law to emerge from the prison of the blocks of stone where they remained in the minds of the people. Jesus summarized the Law in terms of love. In order for humans to fulfil their creative purpose they must love God and love others, and this must be reflected in the "rules" governing human behaviour.

Through expression of love, humans progress towards the likeness of God and become creative. Love, Jesus taught, is the very nature of God, and through loving and being loved humans experience God. The human experience of love is our insight into the supernatural, or spiritual, universe. We no longer have to be suspicious of, or embarrassed by, these terms or let their intangibility and metaphysical nature deny their reality. They are vindicated by the human experience of love. Through love our minds can be opened to a greater universe than natural science can view from its limited perspective. This is the life offered by Jesus: not the limited span of our occupation of this planet, but eternal life in the spiritual universe.

The problem with terms such as "harmony" and "love" for the logical thinker is that they cannot be defined precisely and may mean different things to different people. Human progress will inevitably make these concepts clearer, but religion calls us to enter into a relationship with the creator God before all things are clear. It calls us to trust our instincts and to move forward in faith. In the spirit of not leaving definable terms undefined, it is worth looking at what is meant by "faith". Faith is the first step we take in relating to God the creator; and the wisdom of holy scriptures, such as the Old Testament, reveals three aspects of faith. First, there is knowledge of the creator God that comes from observation and experience. Secondly, there is trust, the calmness that comes from submission to a power that is ultimately good. Thirdly, there is interaction with God, because faith is not a docile acceptance of fate, but a daily struggle to find the best way forward in partnership with God in his work of creation.

The creative struggle between short-term self-interest and loving behaviour is seen in the life of Jesus. Accounts tell how he was tempted along paths that led to a comfortable life with worldly power, but that he resisted in order to offer his life to the progress of humanity. This was a path that made his death inevitable as he challenged the religious and secular authorities of the day. Jesus gave his life following a path that was both sacrificial and creative; he could do no other thing. Although the humanity in Jesus struggled to find a way to avoid the pain and separation of physical death, Jesus acted out of love for all humankind when he faced the worldly consequences of being the Word made flesh.

This enabled the death of Jesus to redefine death for us. Yes, it was death in scientific terms, because science operates within time and space, but it was not death in the wider dimensions in which God is found. The death of Jesus has revealed death as a portal to these other dimensions that cannot be experienced in this life. We are given a glimpse of this new and eternal life through the projection of the Word of God back into time and space after the death of Jesus. He was seen by many witnesses at the time, but the bodily resurrection of Jesus exceeds our ability to provide a scientific rationalization. It was, however, witnessed and believed by many at the time, and history shows how it strengthened and invigorated the embryonic Christian Church. The new life outside of time and space is shown to be available to all humans through the first human to make that journey, Jesus of Nazareth—the Word of God in human form.

. . . and the life was the light of all people

Jesus of Nazareth is the "Word made flesh", but he is also the existence of God outside of our physical universe, whose pouring out of himself in creation is the greater reality to which Jesus testifies. The life of Jesus reveals to us the spiritual nature of human beings. Jesus, describing himself as the Son of Man, lived a life that was consistent with his unity with God. The influential twentieth-century Protestant theologian Paul Tillich (1886–1965) expresses this as Jesus not being different from humankind "except insofar as he fully reveals God within his own finitude". Through his teaching and healing, Jesus brought enlightenment and comfort to many, and he established a Church to continue his work after his death.

Important as his life was, his greatest teaching came through the manner of his death. Jesus remained true to the principles which he taught, and died in obedience to God's creative direction. His willingness to die to show humankind the path to their potential future in unity with God is a staggering act of love.

The Church has viewed this self-sacrificial death in many ways, and the various doctrines that describe the death of Jesus as atoning for the shortcomings of humankind seek to reveal the power of Jesus's decision to offer himself for death in this way. There are explanations from the legal viewpoint, which describe Jesus as accepting the punishment for our wrong choices, symbolized by Adam's disobedience. There are commercial arguments on Jesus paying the price of our freedom from slavery: that is our slavery to self-indulgence. There are also arguments that relate to the tradition of sacrifice in primitive religions. All of these have something to say to us, but they are not particularly helpful in understanding our journey to fulfil our destiny.

An explanation of the death of Jesus that directs our vision to the future, rather than dwells on the mythologized shortcomings of the past, comes from the French mediaeval theologian and monk Peter Abelard (1079–1142). Abelard was a controversial figure, remembered mostly for his ill-fated love for his pupil, Héloise, and he was criticized by the Christian establishment of the time for applying reason to matters of faith. Hmmmm.

Abelard argued that Jesus's death is an act of love which causes us to respond in love for God. God in turn responds to our love with forgiveness, and Abelard sees this as the way that Jesus atones for our failures to be as creative as we can be. This *moral theory of atonement* is more helpful with continuing creation than the mainstream doctrines surrounding Jesus's death, because it calls us to respond by following the example of love that Jesus has set.

Abelard's moral theory shows Jesus illuminating the path of spiritual maturity. Through his life, his teaching and his actions we see a person who is totally human and at the same time is part of a greater and unseen existence. Although it is unseen by us, this greater reality is sensed. Jesus is recognized by Christians as the pattern of their destiny, and the example of his life and his teachings maps the way to achieving that destiny.

Through this, Jesus illuminates the reality of our being.

. . . he gave power to become children of God

Fasten your seat belts for a bumpy ride!

Metropolitan John Zizioulas (1931–2023), a theologian from the Eastern Orthodox Church, postulated how humans can progress from the individuality of creaturely existence into our full potential, which he termed *personhood*. Individual *being* is achieved at birth, but personhood can only be attained in relationship to God. Personhood, unlike our biological being, is not limited in time and space, and it involves us in *de-individualization*. Metropolitan John helped us to understand that true personhood is achieved through becoming an irreplaceable part of a community that is not bounded by time and space.

You may, or may not, find Metropolitan John's metaphor of attaining personhood easier to understand than John the Evangelist's description of our right to become children of God. The important point is that they both point to our God-given potential of an existence in another dimension, which we call the spiritual world. In this world, we are part of a community that is related to the Creator in the same way that the Word of God and the Spirit of God relate to the Creator.

It is difficult to comprehend the enormity of this potential for each of us, but this was made possible by Jesus Christ. Christians believe that Jesus was born with full personhood: he recognized himself to be a corporate entity, destined to draw the many into himself. The gateway to *de-individualization* is the Church that Jesus founded, where we can be born into the new life leading to personhood through baptism and be sustained as we mature spiritually and progress from the image of God to the likeness of God.

I said that it wouldn't be easy!

To summarize, the *logos*, or Word of God, is the concept that allows us to visualize the potential of creation at the moment of the Big Bang, rather as the genetic material in a newly fertilized egg contains the potential for the fully grown adult. The egg is not a blueprint for the mature adult and its achievements, because external factors will influence the development of the egg, but the genetic material opens a whole range of possibilities. It also limits possibilities in that a hen's egg cannot grow into a duck. The Word of God in the form of a human being, or the "Word made flesh", reveals the potential of human beings to grow into the likeness of God. Jesus of Nazareth is understood by Christians to be the gateway to this eternal and corporate existence in another dimension.

The Word of God does not, however, explain what has driven, and continues to drive, creation forward to realize its potential. There is another dimension to creation that arises from theology that describes the driving force of creation or God at work in the universe. It is the concept of the "Spirit of God".

PART 3

The creative force

A wind from God swept over the face of the waters.
Genesis 1:2

... and I have filled him with divine spirit, with ability, intelligence, and knowledge in every kind of craft.
Exodus 31:3

... for God knows that when you eat of it your eyes will be opened, and you will be like God, knowing good and evil.
Genesis 3:5

At that time people began to invoke the name of the Lord.
Genesis 4:26

A wind from God swept over the face of the waters

The Genesis creation story has the mysterious image of the "Spirit of God" moving in creation. God creates through utterance, but the "Spirit" of God is present in creation, fashioning it according to God's Word. This metaphysical representation of the *modus operandi* of the creator adds a new dimension to the nature of creation. This can be called the spiritual domain or the supernatural, but whatever it is called, it falls outside of current scientific knowledge. The concept of the "Spirit of God" can, however, be expanded logically in the light of observations of our world, but I think that I need to warn that the arguments become increasingly abstract as we approach the interface of creation and the creator.

The Word of God and the Spirit of God provide, respectively, a potential and an ongoing creative force in the universe. The fundamental nature of matter and the forces that act upon it can be taken as evidence of that potential, because the universe would not have evolved from the Big Bang without them. Indeed, the Big Bang itself could not have happened without there being a set of physical conditions that permitted it.

The historic growth of complexity in the created universe to the point of the development of life from matter testifies to the creative force. Increasingly complex systems behave according to more and more complex rules, and the creative force can be seen as driving the expansion of the rule book as creation evolves and moves forward. The previous example of the rules of chemistry emerging as chemical elements were formed illustrates this. The rules that applied to matter before the formation of the elements clearly allowed for the rules of chemistry, so we can say that they were a design option. The rules were, however, observable only after matter had cooled and condensed into atoms, and emerged as more elements were generated in the nuclear factories of the stars. Each new law of nature articulated by humankind's scientific discoveries seems to be a milestone marking the progress of creativity in the universe.

It is intriguing to consider whether the creative force can be characterized using existing mathematics and physics. Is there an as yet undiscovered fundamental particle (the *agapon*?) which mediates the creative force? Is a creative force hiding in the indeterminacies of quantum theory or chaos theory? In the absence of a physical characterization of the creative force, a physical explanation is, to say the least, unlikely. At present even the well-characterized fundamental force of gravity is not fully understood, and a quantum gravitational theory is still required in pursuit of unification of the fundamental forces of nature. And of course there's dark energy and dark matter, which we observe from its effect on the expansion of the universe, but we cannot yet define.

We can learn more about the creative force by looking at its consequences in the world we experience. Human creativity and insight may be a route to understanding the force on which it depends, but there are dangers of circular arguments here. A safer starting point for an exploration of the creative force is the process of biological evolution, which allows us to study creation on a more human scale. Natural selection is a mechanism that science has identified in biological evolution, and it is worth examining the characteristics of this observable phenomenon in pursuit of the nature of the creative force.

The mechanism of natural selection can be reduced to three essential components. First, there needs to be a number of competing futures for natural selection to work on, and this is known as variation. Variation in a species is caused by a number of mechanisms that introduce changes to the genetic material. Sexual reproduction mixes genetic material from individuals, but there are other ways in which genetic variation can occur, such as mutation due to the effect of radiation on DNA.

Secondly, natural selection needs a competitive environment for variants in a species. If a red beetle species produces a variant that is green, the green beetle will be less conspicuous on a leaf and therefore be less likely to be eaten by a bird. The green beetle has been given an advantage through whichever mechanism caused the initial variation. In this case a predator, the bird, provides the competitive environment, but the competition could equally be provided by a shortage of food or many other environmental factors.

The third feature of natural selection is that it builds on success. Heredity is the mechanism in natural selection that enables successful variants to flourish. Our green beetle lives longer, lays more eggs and, essentially, can pass on its gene for greenness to the next generation. Because of its natural advantage, the green beetle eventually becomes more populous than the red beetle.

A question arises as to whether the whole process of natural selection can be used to characterize the creative force, or whether the creative force influences one part of the process particularly. The generation of variants would be an obvious place to look for the effects of the creative force, because, once variation occurs, the second and third stages are an inevitable consequence of placing variants in the same environment. This inevitability only exists because of the natural laws that govern the behaviour of matter and energy in the universe, so it can be seen that the creative force and the creative potential, or the Word of God and the Spirit of God, are inseparably linked. I will, therefore, persevere with a holistic view of natural selection as a creative process under the influence of a creative force.

In our example, the green beetle is more adapted for survival in its environment than the red beetle. This could also be expressed in metaphysical terms as the green beetle existing in greater harmony with its environment. Creation has already been described as a movement in the direction of greater complexity, but natural selection helps us also to see it in terms of a movement towards harmony. This movement is not a benign drift but a violent struggle, as it occurs in an environment of competition and predation. Death is a necessity for this process to work and for organisms better adapted to their environment to emerge.

From natural selection, we get a view of the creative force as a movement in the direction of harmony with the broader environment, but we also see this as operating through struggle and death as potential futures are tested at the very edge of oblivion.

. . . and I have filled him with the divine spirit

After that sobering view of the creative force from natural selection it may now be safe to look at human creativity. The Bible offers some early examples of human creativity which harnesses the creative force. The book Exodus (Chapter 31) describes the exceptional skills and artistry required to decorate the Ark of the Covenant achievable through a man, Bezalel Son of Uri, inspired by the Spirit of God. Earlier, in the book Genesis, Joseph's exceptional visionary gifts are attributed to the presence of God's Spirit.

A person's interaction with the creative force, the Spirit of God, raises the question of the relationship between the brain and the mind, which continues to be a live issue among philosophers. Dualism and monism are the two major schools of thought, each encompassing a range of ideas. Dualism can be traced back to Plato, but it is now associated with the seventeenth-century philosopher René Descartes (1596–1650). Dualists argue for a separate existence of the mind and the brain. Monism can also trace its roots back to the Ancient Greeks but is generally associated with another seventeenth-century philosopher, Baruch Spinoza (1632–77). Monists do not see the brain and the mind as separate entities. The development of increasingly powerful artificial intelligence (AI) provides ammunition to both sides of the debate, but progress to date has not, to me, demonstrated that the function of the mind has been created outside of the human body. I'm watching this one closely!

If the mind–body problem is still the subject of intense speculation in philosophical and scientific circles, then the introduction of a spiritual element, the human soul or spirit, presents a whole new bunch of difficulties to rational enquiry. Some find no distinction between the mind and the spirit, but the eighteenth-century rationalist philosopher Immanuel Kant (1724–1804) separates his outer world sense, which connects him in wonder to the glories of creation, from an inner moral sense by which he is connected to the infinite.

The human soul is, to the Christian, a term to describe the essence of a person that is associated with the body and mind during life and survives the death of the body. The soul is, therefore, not a physically derived human property, and is best described in terms of morality and spirituality. This concept can also be traced back to Socrates and Plato. Generally speaking, scientific thought does not distinguish between the mind and the soul and seeks an explanation for the mind in the physiology and chemistry of the human brain.

If the soul is the eternal component of the human condition, related to mind and body in the lifetime of a person, then it is logically the means by which the mind can interact with the creative force.

The influence of the creative force pervades the history of human endeavour. We speak of "inspiration" at moments of creativity or insight, and this terminology reflects a widely held feeling that human intellect is interacting with the creative force, or the Spirit of God. Is there a better explanation for the insights of the early philosophers in the pre-scientific age, or indeed for the deep truths in the book Genesis, some of which have been subsequently supported by scientific enquiry? The progress of science itself is not just a plodding march of discovery; instead it moves forward in bursts following flashes of inspiration. Ideas from inspired thinkers such as Plato, Copernicus, Newton, Darwin and Einstein catch fire in the scientific community and stimulate new waves of enquiry which illuminate the dark corners of human understanding.

Describing human creativity as making decisions that are harmonious with the direction of the creative force, however true, is an unduly prosaic statement of a wonderful and exciting reality. The true excitement of human creativity is experienced on a higher plane when the creative force is involved. Such creativity stimulates not only the creative person, but all those who fall within the sphere of the work of creation. We continue to enjoy the work of great mathematicians, musicians, artists, philosophers and poets, and there are many other fields of creativity that elevate the human spirit and move humanity forward in the direction of becoming the likeness of God.

Many creative individuals have spoken of experiencing the creative force. Some refer to it as a force within themselves that wells up as they work; others feel it as an external force. The pianist Arthur Rubinstein spoke of "this thing in us, a metaphysical power that emanates from us". In concerts, he often felt an energy reaching out from himself into the audience. "It is something floating, something unknown that has no place to disappear to." In his Nobel Prize acceptance speech, novelist Saul Bellow declared, "The sense of our real powers, powers we seem to derive from the universe itself, also comes and goes. We are reluctant to talk about this because there is nothing we can prove, because our language is inadequate, and because few people are willing to risk talking about it. They would have to say that there is a spirit, and that is taboo."

Yes, Mr Bellow, taboo to many, but religious people are not reluctant to talk about spirituality. The language of science is of little help in exploring these experiences because the creative force is not a field of serious scientific enquiry. Explanations from science tend to be evolutionary and reductionist, as scientists explore the intricacies of the development and operation of the brain chemistry that gives rise to spiritual feelings. Religion, however, is the holistic exploration of spiritual instincts and experiences, and the major world religions represent the wisdom and experience collected over many generations.

Science is hampered in its work by a view that everything in creation is accessible, given time, to the unassisted human brain. Given the tremendous progress that science has made to our understanding of the origins and nature of the universe, it is easy to see how science can be seduced into this position. This is, however, an arrogant attitude if it does not consider whether the progress of human knowledge is a solely human achievement or whether it has been accomplished by interaction of the human mind with the creative force.

Christianity has no doubts here and has developed a vocabulary to explain it. God is known through his self-revelation in creation, through his creative *logos* in human form and through the ongoing inspiration we receive from the creative force. It is through the creative force that we are in partnership with God in the continuing process of creation, which has a goal of the universe in harmony as humankind grows into the likeness of God. This is a movement of humanity in the direction of community as our individualities unite in God's masterplan, the divine *logos*.

The Christian view can explain the experience of inspiration, creativity and spirituality. Our minds, made in the image of God, are hard-wired with creative directionality and with the ability to interact with the creative force. Creativity, therefore, has both an internal and an external component which, I believe, corresponds with most people's instincts and feelings on creativity once the need is removed for an explanation in terms of current scientific knowledge.

Religious enquiry into the nature of God, God's relationship to humankind and its destiny, can be seen as the same process of interaction of the human mind and the creative force. Religion too has produced its luminaries who have sparked waves of doctrinal development. Religion is a basic instinct of humanity, and it is too easy to dismiss it as superstition because science has not yet been able to design an experiment to test it and articulate it in a natural law. Our ability to see the beauty of creation, and the wonders of our natural world, speak of our interaction with the creative force. We are uplifted and invigorated by music and the other arts through our interaction with the creative force. Indeed, appreciation of the beauty of creation, whether God's creation or that inspired in humans, elevates us as our thoughts harmonize with the creative force, and this feeling of harmony with all of creation is the basis of religion.

Ironically, the concept of a creative force as an inspiration for the development of the scientific method of enquiry will create a problem for people for whom science is regarded as the only route to enlightenment. This blind spot is just as much a handicap as that carried by the fundamentalist who rejects scientific discoveries that contradict a literal reading of a religious text. I do have sympathy with the sceptical scientist who can point to past instances where the "God of the gaps" has been invoked to explain a phenomenon that later turned out to have a natural explanation, but science too has had its own shaky constructs. The "aether" was postulated as the medium to carry light waves before new theories on the nature of light rendered it unnecessary. The mysterious substance "phlogiston" was sought to explain combustion before the role of oxygen was discovered by Antoine-Laurent Lavoisier (1743–94). The concept of a creative force does not fall into this category because it provides an explanation of insight that pre-dates science. Also, science is not seeking an explanation for evolution of the complexity of the universe outside of applying statistical rules to random changes over billennia; a sort of "Big Bang bingo", whose outcome will at best only reveal another mechanism of creation without giving insight into cause or purpose.

In the euphoria of experiencing the creative force in our own work or in the work of others, we must not forget the lesson from natural selection that creativity works at the edge of oblivion. Death and suffering are a necessary part of the human condition, and one of the biggest challenges to religion is to reconcile human suffering with a view of an all-powerful God whose nature is love. The progress of ongoing creation, and the bigger picture that this gives of the role of humanity in the process, opens up a way of understanding the vicissitudes of human life. The creative role of humankind brings us face-to-face with the evil of suffering, disharmony, chaos and oblivion. But before it all sounds too bleak, we must allow a view of the bigger picture to allow it to make sense. The life and death of Jesus of Nazareth shows us the creative power of sacrificial love in the face of evil. The Gospels tell how Jesus showed in the most graphic way that death is not necessarily the final outcome for humans; indeed that it can, through the Spirit of God, become the door to a greater reality.

... you will be like God, knowing good and evil

We have explored the nature of the creative process as one of building upon success. In biological evolution, heredity allows successful adaptations of an organism to its environment to be carried through to successive generations. Although this could at first be viewed as a mechanical process set in progress by God the creator and left to run to its inevitable conclusion, this view ceases to be tenable at the point where the created universe becomes aware of itself. This point of creation's self-awareness was reached with the evolution of human consciousness, or sapience. It was the eighteenth-century Swedish naturalist Carl Linnaeus (1707–78) who first included humankind in his classification of nature, and he decided that sapience, or wisdom, was the defining characteristic when he named the human species, *Homo sapiens*.

The Genesis myth of the Garden of Eden is concerned with this moment in evolutionary history when a self-aware and sapient species emerged. Adam and Eve, representing the first man and woman, disobediently reach out for the knowledge that is God's: the knowledge of good and evil. Having this knowledge means that they are no longer innocent but are now accountable for their own decisions. Genesis describes this in the metaphor of their expulsion from the Garden of Eden.

It is difficult to overstate the importance of this critical moment in the history of the observed universe. A species, humankind, has emerged which is able to choose between good and evil: to follow a path in harmony with the creative force or in disharmony. The age of innocence is over and a new phase of creation has begun. The evolutionary point mythologized by the Garden of Eden puts humankind in the frontline of creation, face-to-face with death and oblivion.

A new tool of creation has emerged in the ability of humans to acquire knowledge and to make choices in harmony or disharmony with the creative force and in the direction of the creative potential. Creative decisions are those which are harmonious with the *logos*, or the Word of God. They lead to good rather than bad, to creation rather than chaos. Human history tells that the right choices are not always made, and that there are catastrophic consequences. The stories in the book Genesis describe how God intervenes to curb the excesses of human behaviour, but ultimately preserves human free will and creativity.

Harmonious and creative decisions have been represented in many ways in religious texts. They certainly involve selflessness, where an individual decides on a path that is consistent with their beliefs and is to the benefit of others rather than themselves. This is represented by Jesus's summary of the law: to love God and to love your neighbour as yourself, which can be taken as a call to be creative. But there is another dimension to this which involves personal sacrifice. Human understanding of sacrifice has developed from the ancient practice of ritual sacrifice to appease God to an understanding of sacrifice as a creative process through self-giving. Sacrificial behaviour moves creation forward and is humankind working in partnership with God towards creation's goal. Through self-sacrifice we foreshadow our destiny as a corporate entity.

Adam and Eve are representative of the whole of humankind and its ability to reproduce, and human creativity is both an individual and a species-wide phenomenon. Each generation adds to the cumulative pool of human knowledge, revising and refining it in the light of the progress of ideas from new observations and thought. Initially this was achieved through the oral tradition, but later came art, writing and information technology. This is analogous to heredity in the process of natural selection because it enables creative success to be passed on to the next generation. Through the transmission of learning from one generation to the next we stand on top of a column of knowledge that dates back to that "Garden of Eden moment".

... people began to call on the name of the LORD

The human brain is the most complex manifestation of the process of natural selection. It is the organ which monitors and regulates bodily functions, responding to sensory information which it receives and processes. Different areas of the brain are associated with different brain functions. In the human brain, the frontal lobes of the cerebral cortex are greatly expanded, and these are associated with reasoning and abstract thought. It is through evolution of the brain that humankind has emerged as a species. The human sapience identified by

Linnaeus is an abstract concept with physical, mental and spiritual components.

Controversies continue to rage around the respective contributions of nature and nurture in continuing human development, and new branches of science such as evolutionary biology and evolutionary psychology are exploring how the principles of natural selection can apply in the acquisition of human knowledge. Political and sociological dogma (yes, it's not only the Church that is guilty of dogma!) have made it difficult to accept a genetic component to personality, intelligence and the acquisition of knowledge, but scientific opinion generally views the "nature versus nurture" debate as a meaningless distinction. After all, nurture, considered in the broader sense that encompasses all environmental factors, is a component of natural selection and therefore genetic development. Studies on twins separated at birth demonstrate many personality traits in common in the adults, and the genetic contribution is undeniable.

Receptivity to the creative force, mediated by the soul and processed by the mind, is a characteristic of the physiology and chemistry of the brain, and is a heritable trait. The creative giants of history have benefited from this gift from their ancestry, but that does not leave the rest of us looking on with envy, or, worse still, leaving creativity up to others.

Receptivity to the creative force can be enhanced through techniques which have been developed over the centuries. Religious rites, worship and prayer are all such techniques, but there are many other spiritual approaches that people can adopt to suit their own genetically and culturally hard-wired pre-dispositions and preferences. These ways of "tuning in" to the creative force form part of the acquired pool of wisdom of humankind and serve an important creative purpose. The ancient Celtic Christians saw God in the design of the sky, the seas, the hills, the forests and all things natural. These were not God in a pantheistic sense, but their spiritual nature revealed God. Particular places made them feel closer to God, and they called these "thin places". Rowan Williams (b. 1950) writes of times when the world is sometimes "a bit more transparent" to the underlying act of God, which he sees as "steady swell of a loving presence". These are expressions of humankind reaching out for God or "tuning in" to the creative force.

Prayer is a conscious effort to engage the creative force. It can be described as a conversation with God, but most people would see it as an experience beyond words involving the praying person at a deep, emotional level. This is sometimes called communion with God. Prayer is an activity which enables people to maintain their lifestyle according to their beliefs. It strengthens the person and orientates them along a path consistent with their faith: it enables them to acknowledge their detours along inappropriate paths and to be able to put their inconsistent behaviour behind them. Praying for divine intervention in situations demonstrates faith that the creative force, and hence God, is experienced at a personal level. The act of praying for an outcome, for themselves or for others, engages the creative force and enables it to act through the people praying: creativity is unleashed to take the situation to a good outcome.

Ritual, worship and other spiritual disciplines are all devices to engage the creative force. Worshippers are inspired by words, music, art, dance—indeed by all the manifestations of the creative force working in humankind. Inspiration comes also from the beauty of creation, and, for Christians, from the life and teaching of Jesus of Nazareth, the *logos* in human flesh. As in prayer, there is comfort and orientation from feeling the nearness of the creator. Worship is also a collective activity, and it gathers people together in a common purpose and begins to form them into a synergistic group who can strengthen and support each other in living out their faith.

The creative force helps an individual to discern courses of action that are creative, while the unaided human mind might choose a more selfish and less strategic path. This often results in mental struggles within an individual. As St Paul wrote, "For I do not do the good I want, but the evil I do not want is what I do" (Romans 7:19). St Paul describes the selfish action as sin, and the "good" is the action in harmony with the creative force. He has a better track record than most at making creative decisions, but even he is reduced to despair by the inner struggle between selfish needs and the desire to be in harmony with the creative force—the Spirit of God.

But people do not have to be religious to experience the creative force, just as you don't have to believe in gravity to fall out of a tree. Any activity that harnesses the creative force is life-enhancing and beneficial in a strategic sense. There may be a price to pay in terms of the short-term needs and desires of the individual, but this is highly rewarded in the long-term development of the individual and society. Christians believe that Jesus of Nazareth gave the ultimate example of creative, sacrificial behaviour when he pursued a path that led to his own destruction. The story of his temptation in the wilderness shows that he was aware of alternatives that offered more short-term rewards at lower risk, but the *logos* of God chose the path that was consistent with his nature and in the direction of the creative force. Even with Jesus the temptation to follow the path of self-interest is never far away. We read of the intensity of his struggle to follow the direction of the creative force in the Garden of Gethsemane, where he prayed "until his sweat was like drops of blood falling to the ground". He chose God's way, which led to his torture and execution. Just as in natural selection, human creativity is ultimately a struggle at the edge of death.

The creative force, then, offers an explanation of the success of pre-scientific insights into the nature of humankind and the universe, and it continues to inspire scientific and philosophical enquiry. Humankind can make leaps of imagination through viewing human experience through the lens of the creative force and be affirmed in the knowledge of "right" and "wrong" through feeling harmony or disharmony with the *logos*. The religious instinct within humankind is the intrinsic receptivity to the creative force. Denial of this instinct through humanistic or secularist philosophy closes a door to insights that humans are created to experience and need to have in order to fulfil their potential in creation. The pictorial mythology that arises from these insights must, however, be treated for what it is. It is an expression of the truth that will be refined by greater knowledge and understanding. It is an eternal truth expressed for a generation, and, as such, it needs to be reinterpreted in each generation.

The implications of humankind being at the "bleeding edge" of creation in our known part of our known universe affect all people, whether they think about these matters or not. People want a fulfilling life, and they seek happiness for themselves and those they love. Happiness is often pursued along the path of self-gratification or in the direction of accumulating wealth or through achievement of power or celebrity, and this is despite the abundant examples of unhappiness, disillusionment and tragedy that result. True fulfilment can involve all of the above, but it has the essential requirement of harmony with the creative force, which can be seen by the love that we show in our lives. We are in an age of staggering human achievement in terms of investigation of the natural universe. Humankind has applied its discoveries in the invention of new technologies with great creative potential and, therefore, great destructive power. This has resulted in a certain intellectual arrogance in our age where the wisdom of the past is too quickly dismissed and God increasingly becomes irrelevant in people's thoughts. Thinking itself is becoming corrupted for many who rely on the mass media to feed them opinions on global matters. All well and good as long as the media they rely on are driven by a desire to publish the truth and are not primarily motivated by the desire for money and power through feeding the baser instinct for self-gratification of their consumers. The arrogance of our age has resulted in a gap between our power to affect our environment and our ability to harness the creative force to use that power creatively. This represents a great danger to the human race.

A creative life must be based on a continuous pursuit of harmony with the creative force. Religion offers a structure for this, but the world religions must wake up to the fact that they are failing to interpret their message for the present age. Jesus of Nazareth called the religious leaders of his time "whitewashed tombs". They stuck to the letter of the ancient law and had not interpreted it to meet the needs of the age. This must be a constant challenge to Christians and those of all religions as they examine how they can help their people lead a creative life in harmony with the creative force.

The creative force, or the Holy Spirit of God, or love, is experienced by all humans, but many remain unaware of the importance of a conscious approach to becoming more attuned to its guidance in all aspects of life.

An example of living in harmony with the creative force is the act of forgiveness. When we are wronged, we have the choice of forgiving the offence and moving on, or of discharging our resentment in bitterness and revenge. The latter course is destructive and perpetuates victimhood, whereas forgiveness is a path to healing and creativity both for the person giving and the person receiving forgiveness. A process of recognition of the offence, reflection on its consequences, remorse on behalf of the offender and a strong desire for forgiveness and a new way forward, is a path to maturity and a movement in the direction of becoming the likeness of a forgiving God. It is the path of love rather than the path of hate.

Allowing love to guide our lives cannot be achieved in isolation, and it requires relationships, communities and a fellow feeling with all humankind. Religious institutions such as churches, synagogues, mosques and temples were established to provide a focus for these communities seeking together a creative life. My experience is of the Christian Church in the Western civilization, where those that have adapted so that they speak to the current age continue to flourish, but those that have stood still face decline and risk having no legacy for future generations. A Church must be creative to survive and to support its members in a creative life. A love and respect for tradition must always be subordinate to the prime purpose for which the Church was founded. It must never become what its founder would describe as a "whitewashed tomb".

The creative journey of humankind from being the image of God to being the likeness of God can be seen as a process of drawing together in a community attuned to the creative force. Our biological nature encourages individualism and self-interest, but we have a creative destiny where our individualism is our gift to a communal humanity which can unite in a deep relationship with God.

This raises the key issue of our human identity. Are we truly important to God as individuals with free will to make creative or destructive decisions, or are we destined to lose all personal identity in a corporate conglomeration of humanity? The visualization of God as a trinity of three persons, Father, Son (*logos*) and Holy Spirit, helps in understanding the apparent contradictions between individuality and a corporate community. In the Gospel of John (10:38), Jesus is quoted as saying "the Father is in me and I am in the Father". This shows us a reciprocal relationship where not only do we contribute our individuality to the community, but our individuality is also enhanced by the relationship. Jesus is also reported by John (14:9) as saying "Whoever has seen me has seen the Father", indicating an emergence of the likeness of God as humankind progresses in the direction of its destiny. Irenaeus offers the image of the Son and the Holy Spirit as the two arms of God by which humanity was made and taken into God's embrace. This image helps us to see the Creative Potential and the Creative Force as the working arms in creation, the embracing arms of love and the gathering arms of inclusion.

PART 4

The end of creation

Then I saw a new heaven and a new earth; for the first heaven and the first earth had passed away; and the sea was no more.
Revelation 21:1

"I am the Alpha and the Omega", says the Lord God, who is and who was and who is to come, the Almighty.
Revelation 1:8

For as all die in Adam, so will all be made alive in Christ.
1 Corinthians 15:22

I have already described how we can know God from his self-revelation in the act of creation, the creative potential and the creative force, which I have related to the Christian trinitarian view of God as Father, Son and Holy Spirit. Science and common sense would strongly suggest that nothing comes from nothing, and the concept of *ex nihilo* creation is difficult to accept. This difficulty disappears if God is seen as creating the universe from himself, and the created universe is acknowledged as part of the substance of God projected into time and space. Our exploration of the material universe through natural science therefore becomes a path to knowing God, or, more accurately, God as manifested in time and space. But where is creation going and what is it for? Surely, the end, as in termination, will reveal the end as in purpose.

For the first heaven and the first earth had passed away

There are many theories on the future, and possible end, of the universe from science. The fate of the universe is delicately balanced. The unknown factors in forecasting the end of creation are the mysterious dark matter and dark energy. Depending on the amount of dark matter and energy in the universe, it could continue to expand until a point is reached where all of its energy is evenly spread over a vast volume of space and there is insufficient energy for any interaction between matter. The temperature of the universe would be just above absolute zero, and there would certainly be no life or continuing creation. This scenario, probably first proposed by the German physicist Hermann von

Helmholtz (1821–94) in the mid-nineteenth century, is known as *heat death*. It would result in God being diminished as the part of him that was a creative universe became inert matter.

Another scenario is that the universe could reach a point where it ceases to expand and begins to contract under the influence of gravity, culminating in a total collapse that takes it back to square one. Observations that the expansion of the universe is continuing to accelerate have made this scenario seem more unlikely in recent years, but, as with the heat death scenario, this *big crunch* possibility is related to the properties of dark matter and dark energy in the universe, which remain unknown to science. The big crunch, or *gnab gib*, appears to be better news for a God, who is, at least, restored to an immanent starting point, but it does make the whole business of creation that gives us the wonder of life on our human and temporal scale seem somewhat pointless on the cosmic scale.

The fate of humankind is on a much shorter timescale than the lifespan of the universe. Philosophy and theology bring their own perspectives on the ultimate fate of humanity. There are many mystical writings about the end of times, and these are no less prone to literalist readings than the book Genesis. The apocalyptic passages in the Bible, particularly the book Revelation, are a magnet for cryptographers, amateur detectives, cultists and charlatans. Speculation on hidden meanings has generated many *isms*, some of which occasionally take a bunch of gullible *ists* to a mountain top to await the end of the world. Nevertheless, the Abrahamic religions envision a point in history where judgement separates good and evil and humanity is transformed as it is united with the divine.

Christianity teaches a future that is the product of the continuing influence of the creative force, where humankind achieves its evolutionary potential and becomes united with God. The potential of humankind is represented by the *logos*, and St Paul writes of us becoming united in Christ where we surrender our individual natures and worldly desires in order to become the people that God wants us to be in full relationship with him. This evolutionary goal results in an enhancement of God through his creation and seems more feasible than an account of the end of time that omits humankind from the equation.

I am the Alpha and the Omega

Partnership in creation between God and humankind generates many potential futures provided that humans have free will to make their individual choices. The Jesuit priest and palaeontologist Pierre Teilhard de Chardin (1881–1955) saw creation evolving to an end, which he called the Omega Point. This requires further evolution of human thought to achieve a super-consciousness which would lead to social integration and *spiritual maturity*, a term which indicates an enhanced ability of the human mind to interact with the creative force.

This super-consciousness was called the noosphere by Teilhard de Chardin, and the concept was first popularized by Vladimir Vernadsky (1863–1945), a Russian geochemist, who saw it as the third phase of development after the geosphere and the biosphere. The creation of the Earth, the geosphere, provided a substrate for biological evolution to introduce a new dimension of complexity in the biosphere. As the emergence of life transformed the geosphere, so the biosphere is entering a new paradigm through the emergence of human cognition. This concept, unlike Darwinian evolution, requires an overarching design principle under which natural selection can operate, and although the noosphere is somewhat speculative at the moment it is a concept which is consistent with evolution according to the *logos* driven by the creative force. This noosphere must have appeared somewhat far-fetched when the idea first emerged, but the developments in information technology at the end of the twentieth century and into the twenty-first century make it seem far less so. Our access to events happening around the world through the news media show how quickly we have moved into an information age.

It could be said that the sharing of knowledge is the characteristic that ensured the emergence of *Homo sapiens* from the evolutionary pressures that caused the extinction of other hominid species. The prevailing view of the evolution of the hominids is that there was a common ancestor in an ape-like animal that walked upright. The first creature that we would recognize as humanoid emerged in Africa some 2 million years ago and is known as *Homo ergaster*. This species spread from Africa to Asia and evolved into a new species *Homo erectus*. It is generally accepted that *Homo sapiens* left Africa 120,000 years ago and existed alongside several other hominid species including *Homo erectus* and *Homo neanderthalis*. These other species lived until about 30,000 years ago but failed to survive changes in the climate caused by events such as the eruption of the Mount Toba supervolcano 76,000 years ago and the last glacial period, which peaked 20,000 years ago. The ability of *Homo sapiens* to compete successfully with these other species for limited food supplies is generally ascribed to their large brain with highly developed areas for language and speech and a large front of the brain allowing for planning and strategy. The ability to plan and communicate enabled the species to work together and develop tools and weapons and even trade, which gave *Homo sapiens* the edge when competing with other hominid species.

Technological advance has made access to collective human knowledge possible for vastly more people. Fundamental to this giant leap forward has been the development of the interconnectivity of computer networks through the use of common protocols to enable the internet. The Transmission Control Protocol and the Internet Protocol (TCP/IP) emerged in the 1970s from the work of American computer scientists Robert Kahn and Vinton Cerf. Information exchange on the internet was made possible through the work of a British computer scientist, Tim Berners-Lee, who devised the worldwide web protocols for information exchange. This framework for information exchange has encouraged billions of people to engage with information sources and to make their own contributions to the developing noosphere. Unfortunately, a lot of the information shared is toxic to the development of the human spirit, frivolous or just crap, but it would be foolish not to recognize the development of the internet and worldwide web as major steps towards the Omega Point.

The evolution of the geosphere and the biosphere has taken place over aeons that are unimaginable to humans from their relatively short lifespan. However, the evolution of the noosphere is occurring on a very human timescale, and it is quite breathtaking how quickly the human fund of knowledge has developed from oral transmission through written records to electronic databases. Human knowledge is no longer constrained by the human memory, filing cabinets, books or libraries. It is available to all, and all are able to contribute their own insights. It might be comforting for some to see the Omega Point as somewhere in the distant future, but this would be to ignore the rapid evolution of the noosphere. The acceleration we perceive in the sphere of human knowledge reflects the phase of the growth of the biosphere which presaged the new age of human sapience. Cosmogenesis has taken place over 10 billion years: and biogenesis over 2 to 3 billion years. The ability of humans to share their thoughts and ideas has, however, developed in the last 50,000 years of the 13.7 billion years of creation.

The noosphere concept also gives us a view of eternity. Life forms in the biosphere will all die, and even the planets and stars of the geosphere have a finite lifetime, but the knowledge and wisdom acquired in the noosphere have the potential for eternity if they can be united in the Creator outside of time and space. If not, they will die with the geosphere and the biosphere. William Shakespeare wrote in his sonnet, of his lover:

> As long as men can breathe or eyes can see
> So long lives this, and this gives life to thee.

The noosphere, united with the Creator, makes him unduly pessimistic!

Jesus of Nazareth and Christian mystics have spoken of the new paradigm that awaits us, using terms such as *the Kingdom of God* and *a new heaven and a new earth* in terms of an imminent event. Imminence is, of course, subjective, and the early Christians expected this apocalypse daily, but change has accelerated to a point where it is increasingly apparent in the scale of human lifetimes that we are near the beginning of a new chapter in the history of the universe.

For as all die in Adam, so all will be made alive in Christ

The super-consciousness of the noosphere as described by Teilhard de Chardin is more, much more, than a shared database. The social integration and spiritual development it entails must also be considered. The free will that humankind enjoys and the consequent sorrows we endure are, as already discussed, essential to humankind reaching spiritual maturity. The premise that the development of *Homo sapiens* is no longer measured by the pace of bio-evolution, but on the much shorter timescale of the growth of human awareness, gives new insight into the life of Jesus of Nazareth, and the message of urgency in his teaching.

A secular position that the spectacular progress of science obviates the need for God in explaining human existence is a monochrome view which is bounded by the physical universe. Religion gives a polychromatic vision of dimensions and powers that lie beyond time and space, yet influence creativity within our universe. The secular position places responsibility for the future of humankind in the hands of human activity and cosmic good fortune. World history and the current geopolitical situation do not suggest a promising future, despite the tireless efforts of many great people, religious and secular, to tackle the great, global problems of environmental damage, poverty, competition for land, mass migration and criminality, among others. In addition to these challenges, future geological and cosmic activity present a risk of further extinction events. The one certainty that a secular view offers an individual, apart from taxation (!), is death.

For the Christian, the birth of Jesus is a critical stage in human development because it creates a fork in the road in the progress of human evolution. Jesus Christ has been described as the "Second Adam" in that he represents the first of a new kind of human. He offers a developmental path of awareness and spirituality that leads to union with God in an eternal domain, which he called the Kingdom of God. Jesus described himself as "The Way" and his early followers were known as "Followers of the Way" more commonly than as "Christians". The alternative path is bounded by time and space and relies on the human will and ingenuity to solve the problems caused by human creativity. The industrial revolution ultimately led to improved living standards for most people but created problems such as global climate change. The harnessing of atomic energy is part of the solution to reducing carbon emissions, but it has created a potential for human self-destruction. The world is currently examining the huge advantages and potential dangers of Artificial Intelligence, and it is a frightening thought that future technological advances could take place in a culture which has diverged from the moral and spiritual values that spring from a relationship with God. Some scientists hypothesize a coming "Technological Singularity", where a self-improving super intelligence would surpass human intelligence and signal the end of the human race. Presumably, such an intelligence would be bounded by time and space and not be able to relate to God. Other technological risks to the future of *Homo sapiens* include molecular nanotechnology and genetic engineering.

We live in a world where "First Adam" humans and "Second Adam" humans coexist. Jesus was upfront about the stark and divisive nature of his message. Those able to accept his teaching would, through their faith, have a path open to them which led to an eternal relationship with God and Jesus. Those unable to accept follow a path to death. It was a message which, he said, would divide friends and families.

Conclusion

The contribution of religion to the development of human knowledge is to broaden our vision of the nature, purpose and destiny of humanity. Science alone is not equal to the task: it tends to produce a narrow and reductionist view of humankind that turns us into hapless vehicles for the transmission of chemicals along a time axis. However, through seeking God we find ourselves, and we discover the stunning truth that we are empowered as creators who function at the leading edge of creation. Furthermore, we are destined for immortality in dimensions outside of time and space as we unite with the Creator of the universe.

The Big Bang is not just a release of a huge amount of energy into nothingness. The energy comes complete with a set of parameters that govern its nature and its behaviour, and, therefore, its potential futures. It can also be seen as an outpouring of God into nothingness. This is a difficult idea for those who see God as unchanging in creation and unchanged by it, but an event such as the Big Bang means that something happened at the beginning of time that brought God into contact with time and space; with order and chaos; and with life and death. Consideration of this issue in recent years has brought about a promising coming-together of science and Christian thought in the concept of *kenosis*. This term derives from the Ancient Greek word used by the Apostle Paul in his letter to the Philippians to describe how Jesus emptied himself to become human. Kenotic theology views God's action in creation as reducing himself or as a pouring-out of himself. Through creation God gives up a measure of power and exclusivity. God's creation ends the divine isolation and provides an "otherness" for God to which God must relate. This willing surrender of power and exclusivity is an act of love.

If we believe that our universe and, ultimately, ourselves reflect an image of God that is projected into time and space, then we must accept that God is by nature not only a creator but is quite possibly an evolving entity. In order for God to be God he must take risks, lose some control and surrender the outcome. We see this in the freedom that we have to make choices which are positive or negative in respect of the direction of creation, and this freedom means that we stand at the edge of creation facing oblivion. The human race is daily acquiring the knowledge to do great good in the world. This same knowledge contains the power to destroy the human race. This is not a comfortable place to be, but it is made not only tenable, but wonderful and fulfilling because God stands with us. The answer to the age-old question as to why God allows suffering is to be found here. Creation requires God to touch chaos, and we, as partners with God in creation, are also subject to the vicissitudes of change and chance. Christian teaching emphasizes how God is a partner with humankind in suffering as well as in creation.

The presence of God who exists outside of time and space is revealed to us in three ways: by the act of creation; by the potential for ongoing creation; and by the creative force driving creation onwards to its completion. We have seen how the creative force operates in the arena of uncertainty and multiple futures. In religious terms, creation is the Spirit of God confronting chaos, or, as pictorially represented in Genesis, the Spirit of God moving across the face of the waters. God as creator, potential and driving force mirrors the trinitarian language of God as Father, Son and Holy Spirit. Creation occurred, in anthropomorphic terms, either because God wanted it to occur or because it was the very nature of God and therefore inevitable. Perhaps there is no difference between these two reasons in reality, but the moment of creation may represent the boundary of scientific knowledge for all creatures of our universe. We can only know God in this way through his impact in time and space, bounded as we are by the dimensions we occupy. C. S. Lewis described the principle of the power of the Higher where, for instance, "solid bodies exemplify many truths of plane geometry, but plane figures no truths about solid geometry".

God, who exists outside of time and space, cannot be represented fully within those dimensions any more than a cube can be represented in plane geometry.

The understanding of humankind as partners in creation with God, and with the potential to become part of God, presents each one of us with a challenge to realize our destiny. This is such an amazing destiny that it takes some absorbing, and many will flinch from the greatness and the responsibility that it confers on our race and on each of us. Human greatness must be understood in humility, because it is not an achievement of humankind alone, but a destiny made possible by God to be achieved in partnership with God. As for the responsibility, we lack neither guidance on how to live a creative life, nor support as we reach outwards to embrace others seeking the common way. Our guidance comes from inspired teachers from the past, whose wisdom occupies the sphere of human knowledge, or noosphere. Christians can claim that the noosphere is directly enriched by the Creator through the life and teachings of Jesus of Nazareth. Our help comes through our ability to relate to the creative force alive in the universe, which the Bible expresses as God's word written in our hearts.

Spiritual maturity comes through each of us realizing the greatness of our inheritance and according our fellow humans the dignity and respect that each person merits. Those who degrade and exploit their fellow humans, who count human life cheaply, or who put their personal needs above the needs of the world, are working in the direction of destruction and not in the creative direction of human destiny. However, many distractions that arise from our incomplete spiritual creation and the wrong turnings that we take through making bad decisions can be used creatively in our spiritual progress, provided that we are aware of our actions and reflect on their consequences.

The story of creation affirms a clear way forward for the human race, although it also shows that setbacks, disasters and suffering will continue to mark the route in this "vale of soulmaking" that John Keats described. As we make the journey together, the human race will become more and more united in purpose and in love. Our Churches and religious communities need to progress rapidly to take their rightful place in leading the process of spiritual unification. In order to do this, they need to become places where the message of creation is made available to all in the language of the age. This message needs constant restatement as science, technology, political theory and wisdom advance.

A strong Church is vital, not just for the continuing progress of the human race, but for its very survival. The expansion of scientific knowledge is constantly increasing humankind's capability for creation or destruction, and the Church brings direction, hope and confidence as we mature to face our responsibilities. If we ever needed reminding that creation occurs at the edge of oblivion, then we only need to look at the growth of the noosphere in the area of technology.

In our quest for knowledge of the building blocks of creation, we have discovered the relationship between matter and energy, and now have the capability of making the Earth uninhabitable through nuclear war. Our technological progress affects the biosphere that protects us from the harsh cosmic environment in which we live, and we are only just beginning to understand the consequences of this impact. Recent decades have brought us huge advances in knowledge of the nature of life itself, and we are rapidly achieving the capability of producing life forms to our own design, as well as modifying evolved life forms. The dangers to the human race from this knowledge, as well as the potential benefits, are enormous.

Science and religion are both giving us the view of humans as creators, and it is the enemies of religion that consign it to a separate sphere of knowledge divorced from the material world and human achievement. But there is also an enemy within the Church that seeks to make it a museum and thereby an easy target for the spiritual flat-earthers.

Religion must inform all areas of contemporary human knowledge, and it must also be informed by them.

The story of creation of the heavens, the Earth and life from science has many gaps, and scientists have further exciting discoveries to make. Perhaps the biggest current challenges are the mystery of so-called "dark matter", which is the most abundant matter in the universe, and the need for a theory to unite the fundamental forces. Nevertheless, condensing the 13.7-billion-year story of creation revealed by science into a few hundred words highlights the staggering creative power that is contained within those basic laws of nature at the beginning of time. The psalmist who wrote, "The heavens are telling the glory of God; and the firmament proclaims his handiwork", didn't know the half of it!

The Genesis account of the creation of the universe is a remarkable insight given the limits of understanding of the observable universe at the time it was written. It is consistent with the picture that science is developing of *ex nihilo* creation that builds in stages, reflected by the days of creation in Genesis, and provides insight into the creative power present at the beginning. Genesis was ahead of science when it was written, and, in terms of its breadth of vision, remains ahead of science today. The inspiration that gave these insights cannot be ignored by scientists any more than the observations and theories of science can be ignored or refuted by religion.

Nevertheless, the gap between science and religion today is a reality which cannot be denied. It arose historically from the inability of the institutional, and politically powerful, Church to respond to new discoveries. The process of doctrinal development is not as agile as the development of scientific theories. Promulgation of discoveries that conflicted with current dogmas represented a bad career move in the fifteenth century CE, and the progress of science was consequently inhibited. In order to flourish, science had to develop its own niche of thinking and create false boundaries in the search of humankind for knowledge and wisdom. The inadequacy of the response of the Church to the Age of Enlightenment caused further disenchantment by those who sought wisdom through rational enquiry, and it widened the gulf between science and religion.

This differentiation became a comfortable piece of conflict-avoidance that suited both science and theology, and it is still supported by many, perhaps even a majority, who see science and religion as Gould's "non-overlapping *magisteria*". Nevertheless, this is a perfectly respectable position which allows the separated disciplines to show mutual respect and to feed off each other, at least in theory. The reality is that it is still quite possible for each discipline to ignore the development of knowledge from the other, or indeed, to deny the necessity of the other. Another obvious disadvantage of this false boundary is that the borderlands become annexed by many "*ists*" in order to stake out the territory of their "*isms*". I am convinced that the time has come to remove false barriers and to embrace the quest for knowledge as a common goal. It is interesting how scientists from Einstein to Hawking are using the term "God" in a figurative sense as their mathematics and physics lead them closer to the moment of creation. Classical science breaks down at the Planck epoch, the very first moments of the Big Bang when the fundamental forces could have been unified, and further progress in understanding the preceding events will require a new methodology, which may be informed by theology.

Genesis introduces the idea of the "Spirit of God" as the projection of the creator into creation, and as a creative force at work in the universe today. A creator God, a creative potential and a creative force represent a basic tenet of Christianity, and this is the root of the doctrines that describe that faith.

EU GPSR Authorized Representative:

LOGOS EUROPE, 9 rue Nicolas Poussin, 17000 La Rochelle, France

contact@logoseurope.eu

www.ingramcontent.com/pod-product-compliance
Lightning Source LLC
LaVergne TN
LVHW051846080426
835512LV00018B/3096